Stilling the Storm

Practice Interpretation

1

ISSN 2048-0431

Forthcoming titles in this series include:

Acts in Practice, edited by John Vincent
Leviticus in Practice, edited by J.W. Rogerson

Deo Publishing

STILLING
THE STORM

Contemporary Responses to Mark 4.35–5.1

Edited by

John Vincent

deo
PUBLISHING

BLANDFORD FORUM

Practice Interpretation series, 1

ISSN 2048-0431

Printed by Henry Ling Ltd, at the Dorset Press, Dorchester, DT1 1HD, UK

British Library Cataloguing-in-Publication data
A catalogue record for this book is available from the British Library

ISBN 978-1-905679-17-1

Contents

Preface

The recent development of Reception Criticism concentrates on the "use and influence" of biblical books through the ages. Two questions arise from this. First, what is the "use and influence" of these passages, not simply in literary terms, but in consequential action and intentional practice? And second, what "use and influence" do these passages actually exert, not in past times but in the lives and discipleship of "users" today?

It is these two questions that we pursue in the "Practical Interpretation" series, of which the present volume is the first. The basic philosophy of Practice Interpretation remains the papers of our previous volume, *Mark: Gospel of Action: Personal and Community Responses* (London: SPCK, 2006). John Riches' Contextual Bible Study (London: SPCK, 2010) follows similar lines.

The July meetings of the Institute for Socio-Biblical Studies continue with Professor John Rogerson as convenor. The Institutes of 2009 and 2010 concentrated on colleagues presenting and working at "Practice Interpretations" of Mark's Storm-Stilling Story, and the end result of that work together is contained in this volume. As Editor, I record my thanks to the contributors for their colleagueship in the project.

Further volumes on individual passages are at present under active preparation. At the Institute of 2010, we also had presentations on *Acts in Practice*, which we hope to publish shortly, and began planning a volume on *John in Practice*, which we are working at during the Institutes of 2011 and 2012.

Colleagues outside our present number are most welcome to come and join us!

John J. Vincent

Urban Theology Unit
March 2011

The Contributors

David Blatherwick trained at Wesley House, Cambridge, spent a year at Göttingen University, and was Assistant Tutor at Wesley College, Headingley. He subsequently served the Methodist Church in a number of inner-city and suburban circuits and the British Council of Churches as Ecumenical Officer of England. He has explored Mark's Gospel with groups in most of the churches he has served and with Adult Education groups. His published works include "The Markan Silhouetter?", *New Testament Studies* 17 (1970-71), pp. 184-92, *This Stab of Fire* (Epworth, Sermons for Today, 1971) and *Adventures in Unity* (British Council of Churches, 1975). The contribution in this book is a brief summary of the argument presented in an as yet unpublished work on the Storm-Stilling Story in Mark.

Christopher Burdon is Canon Theologian of St Edmundsbury Cathedral and Continuing Ministerial Education Adviser for that Anglican diocese. He was formerly a parish priest and Principal of the Northern Ordination Course and has worked extensively with Christian congregations, students and clergy in England and Scotland, especially in biblical interpretation. He is the author of *Stumbling on God: Faith and Vision through Mark's Gospel* (SPCK 1990). Recent publications include "'To the Other Side': Construction of Evil and Fear of Liberation in Mark 5:1-20", *Journal for the Study of the New Testament* 27.2 (2004), "Mark's Gospel and the Politics of Community", in John Vincent, ed., *Mark: Gospel of Action* (SPCK 2006), and an Essay on William Blake in *Oxford Handbook of English Literature and Theology* (OUP 2007).

John D. Davies was for fourteen years a mission priest and University Chaplain in South Africa, during the time when the apartheid system was being created in all its devious cruelty. This did feel like being at a storm-centre of history; the evil of apartheid was clearly something much more powerful than the simple ill-will of a bunch of individuals. Since his enforced move to the UK in 1970, he has observed similar processes at work in an apparently milder climate. As a Bishop in Shropshire, he found that confrontation with demons was an integral part of his ministry. He collaborated with John Vincent in the publication of the studies on Mark's Gospel entitled *Mark at Work* (Bible Reading Fellowship, 1986). His most recent book is a reflection on St Patrick's Breastplate, called *A Song for Every Morning* (Canterbury Press, 2008).

Leslie Francis is currently Professor of Religions and Education within the Warwick Religions and Education Research Unit, University of Warwick. He is also Visiting Professor in the field of practical theology at York St John University, and serves as Canon Theologian at Bangor Cathedral, Wales. His recent books include *Faith and Psychology: Personality, Religion and the Individual* (2005), *Urban Hope and Spiritual Health: The Adolescent Voice* (2005), *British Methodism: What Circuit Ministers Really Think* (2006), and *Gone for Good? Church-Leaving and Returning in the 21st Century* (2007).

Louise Lawrence is lecturer in New Testament Studies and Research Fellow for the South West Ministry Training Course at the University of Exeter. Her major research interests are anthropological approaches to New Testament texts and cultural and contextual implications of reading scripture. She is author of *An Ethnography of the Gospel of Matthew: A Critical Assessment of the Use of the Honour and Shame Model in Biblical Studies* (WUNT 2; Tübingen: Mohr Siebeck, 2003) and *Reading with Anthropology: Exhibiting Aspects of New Testament Religion* (Carlisle: Paternoster Press, 2005), and co-editor with Mario Aguilar of *Anthropology and Biblical Studies: Avenues of Research* (Leiden: Deo Publishing, 2004). Her latest work, *The Word in Place: Contextual Reflections on the New Testament* (London: SPCK 2009) has initiated a number of community readings of the Bible across the South West of England in a wide diversity of contexts (rural, urban, coastal) and amongst a variety of people (the Deaf, Priests).

Susan Miller teaches New Testament Studies on the Christian Studies Distance Learning Programme at the University of Aberdeen. Her thesis *Women in Mark's Gospel* was published by Continuum in 2004, and she is currently writing a book on *Women in the Fourth Gospel*. For the past ten years she has been a member of the Iona Community, and she is interested in interpreting the Bible in relation to issues of social justice. Her recent publications include "The Descent of Darkness over the Land: Listening to the Voice of Earth in Mark

15:33", in *Exploring Ecological Hermeneutics* (ed. N.C. Habel & P. Trudinger; Atlanta: SBL Symposium Series, 2008).

Andrew Parker trained in theology at New College Edinburgh, and went to work for the French Protestant Industrial Mission in 1968 as an unskilled foreign labourer. Deported in 1973 for involvement in political activities "unbecoming in a foreigner", he worked in Glasgow first as a garage mechanic and then as a hospital porter. He began to write, print and publish cartoon-books on the parables (*Digging Up Parables*, vols. I and II; and *Political Parables*). For twenty years, as a hospital porter in the east end of London, he conducted his own biblical research, published in *Painfully Clear: The Parables of Jesus* (Sheffield: Sheffield Academic Press, 1996) and then in books now on his website: *Light Denied: A Challenge to Historians*; and *God of the Marginals: The Biblical Ideology Performed by Jesus*. He has also returned to his cartoons, making his work available on his website: bibleincartoons.com.

Neil Richardson is a retired Methodist minister now living near Ludlow. He was New Testament tutor at Wesley College, Bristol, from 1984 to 2001, and Principal of the college from 1995. Subsequently, he served as minister of Lidgett Park Methodist Church in Leeds, and as President of the British Methodist Conference 2003-04. He continues to teach and to lead study days. Recent books include *Paul for Today* (2009), *John for Today* (2010), and (with George Lovell) *Sustaining Preachers and Preaching* (2011). Earlier books include *Paul's Language about God*, (1994) and *God in the New Testament* (1999).

John Vincent developed the Urban Theology Unit in 1969 as a way to bring together his twin callings of Gospel scholar and urban missioner. The development of British Liberation Theology and Gospel Practice Interpretation are the result. Recent writings include *The City in Biblical Perspective* (with John Rogerson, London: Equinox, 2009) and *A Lifestyle of Sharing* (Sheffield: Ashram Press, 2009). Practice Criticism continues with articles in the *Expository Times*, most recently September 2010 and August 2011, and in a joint publication with Morna D. Hooker, *The Drama of Mark* (London: Epworth, 2010). Further volumes will follow on *Acts in Practice* and *John in Practice*. His edited volume, *Mark: Gospel of Action,* remains the basic text for Practice interpretation.

Ian Wallis was, until recently, Principal of the Northern Ordination Course, following twelve years as Rector of Houghton-le-Spring in the Diocese of Durham. He served his title in Armthorpe, Doncaster, before becoming Chaplain and Director of Studies in Theology at Sidney Sussex College, Cambridge. His passion is for exploring how the original impulse of faith embodied by Jesus and engendered in his earliest followers can enrich discipleship today. Through his preaching and teaching, as well as through specially designed courses and liturgies, congregations are invited to keep Jesus company along Mark's Gospel journey once more and, through doing so, to discover afresh what it means to be a Christian presence. He explores this experimental approach in his contribution to *Mark: Gospel of Action* (London: SPCK, 2006).

Gerald West teaches Old Testament/Hebrew Bible and African Biblical Hermeneutics in the School of Religion and Theology, University of KwaZulu-Natal, South Africa. He is also Director of the Ujamaa Centre for Community Development and Research, a project in which socially engaged biblical scholars and ordinary African readers of the Bible from poor, working-class, and marginalised communities collaborate for social transformation. Among his recent publications are *The Academy of the Poor: Towards a Dialogical Reading of the Bible* (Pietermaritzburg: Cluster Publications, 2003), and an edited volume, together with Musa Dube, entitled *The Bible in Africa: Transactions, Trajectories and Trends* (Leiden: Brill, 2000).

Bongi Zengele is the Co-ordinator of the Solidarity Programme for People Living with HIV and AIDS within the Ujamaa Centre for Community Development and Research. She is an organic intellectual and a community-based activist. She has collaborated on a number of publications, including the following with Gerald West, "Reading Job 'Positively' in the Context of HIV/Aids in South Africa", *Concilium* 4, 2004, pp. 112-24, and "The Medicine of God's World: What People Living with HIV and Aids Want (and Get) from the Bible", *Journal of Theology for Southern Africa* 125, 2006, pp. 51-63.

Alan Saxby is a supernumerary Methodist minister who, after a period in circuit ministry, moved into a senior ministry post as Counsellor at Barnsley College of Further Education. In active retirement, he is currently completing a PhD in biblical studies at the University of Sheffield with a dissertation on "James (the brother of Jesus) and the Origins of the Jerusalem Church".

1

A Story Alive Today

JOHN VINCENT

The story of Jesus stilling the storm may not be the most obvious source of answers to the question: What are contemporary disciples today finding in Gospel stories that actually motivates, supports or empowers them in discipleship or community activity? However, as this volume shows, study of the story can be surprisingly fruitful in a community context.

The experience and expectation that Gospel stories can legitimate, create or empower disciple practice today is receiving interesting confirmation, as a method. The first part of this piece therefore summarises some of that experience and promise. The second part then begins to open up some of the special issues related to the storm stilling passage. The third part prepares the reader for the journeys with our various contributors in their own particular "takes" on the passage, and mentions some of the "takings".

Then, in the fourth part, there are some hopefully useful suggestions about how the reader, preferably with some friends, could open up the storm stilling story as a source for their own discovery and practice. The methods could be used for other passages, of course.

1. Practice Interpretation

Practice Interpretation is basically an endless series of attempts to write down some of the "calls" in terms of actions, or ideas, or campaigns, or movements, or understandings which disciples see as being derived from, inspired by, supported in, or coherent with, a particular Gospel passage.

The argument for Practice Interpretation, and studies of the various elements, are found in our previous book on *Mark: Gospel of Action*.[1] The background to its emergence in relation to various theological and scriptural studies of the last two decades is in a booklet, *Gospel Practice and Interpretation*.[2]

In one sense, Practice Interpretation is a contemporary collection of "Reception History" exhibits. Reception History widens the boundary of biblical interpretation by encountering the rich variety of biblical interpretations that have emerged in widely differing times and contexts, and through the Bible passages being used for widely differing purposes and projects. Thus, in Christine Joynes's words,

> We can celebrate the plurality of past interpretations as testimony to the dynamic nature of the biblical text; at the same time we are also confronted with the ambiguity of the Bible. The reception history of Mark reveals fascinating ways in which gaps in the text have been filled by different interpreters. The motives, actions and consequences of features that are implicit or unspecified in the biblical text are elaborated in a vast number of directions.[3]

What Practice Interpretation adds to Reception Interpretation is simply the present tense. Reception Reading is concerned with the ways in which, over the centuries, a piece of scripture has been received and used for discipleship, or lifestyles, or projects, or worship, or theology, or movements. Practice Reading is interested in what discipleship, lifestyles, projects, worship, theology and movements that contemporary people today are involved with may derive in some way from the passage in question.

Practice Interpretation attempts to follow the natural instinct of people who hear or read Gospel stories.

If the Gospel is being read as the personal choice of the reader, a number of possible ends or purposes may be in view. The reader may be studying the passage in the context of a church or university training course or degree, or preparing to teach it or preach on it.

In some Charismatic congregations, there is a tension between the "literal" understanding of a passage, and "Spirit-led" ones. Andrew Village has examined the methods that 26 contemporary Anglican church-people have used for reading and responding to the Gospel. He

---

[1] *Mark: Gospel of Action: Personal and Community Responses*, ed. John Vincent, London: SPCK, 2006.

[2] John Vincent in *Outworkings: Gospel Practice and Interpretation*, Sheffield: Urban Theology Unit, 2005. The booklet consists of articles first published in *Expository Times*, including one by John Riches, pp. 28-32.

[3] Christine Joynes, "Reception History", in *Mark: Gospel of Action*, pp. 26-29 (p. 28).

suggests that "perhaps the key ethical demand is that we use what we have to enhance what we are". The "burying your talents" of the parable (Luke 19.11–27; Matt 25.14–30) is "to ignore or avoid the risky business of using who you are, or what you have, when you interpret the Bible". Such (safe) reading is not Kingdom reading because it is too fearful and not faithful. "The master expects us to take risks and to return to him more than he gave us."[4]

Village concludes:

> If this parable is used to shape an empirical theology of scripture, then it speaks of a kind of reading that is unafraid to accept the God of individual differences, unafraid to bring our individuality to the encounter with scripture and unafraid to be changed by that encounter. In many ways, this is totally unlike the kind of reading so long championed by the academy. It is the sort of reading that the academy is beginning to understand as carrying intellectual honesty and virtue. It is the sort of reading that perhaps comes naturally to ordinary Bible readers.[5]

Sometimes, the hearers of the Gospel stand up to listen to it. They might hear the statement, "This is the Gospel of Christ", and answer, "Praise to the Lord". The idea of a "word" is usually understood as being something which is said by one person to another. In this case, the person speaking the word is "the Lord". The authority figure, the speaker of the word, is Jesus of Nazareth, who is felt to be communicating something of value or significance to a group of people who are taken to be his disciples, or at least have put themselves in a place where a "word" from Jesus' story is expected to be heard by contemporary people as something which is meant to be important to them, and from which they expect to get something useful for their own lives.

"The Master is here and calls for you", from John 11.28, is woven on to a colourful frontal placed on the lectern at one church I know. "Do whatever He tells you", from John 2.5, is woven on a pulpit fall in another church I know. Banners in churches proclaim, "Master, speak, thy servant heareth", or "Come, follow me", or "I will make you fishers of people". Plainly, Jesus is thought of as communicating things to disciples which they think they are supposed to put into practice.

---

[4] Andrew Village, *The Bible and Lay People*, Aldershot: Ashgate Press, 2007, p. 167.
[5] Village, p. 168.

Many readings of a Gospel passage are followed by an "exposition", address, or sermon. Typically, after some enlargement on the context, situation or purpose of the passage within the Gospel book, its significance for early hearers will be described, and then its use by contemporary ones will be opened up. Often, two questions predominate:

- First, what does this passage mean, in terms of our beliefs or convictions, or attitudes, or inner dispositions, today?
- Second, what does this passage mean in terms of our relations to others, or things we might do in community, in local life, in politics, today?

It is this second question that is of particular interest to us in Practice Interpretation. Indeed, we sometimes find that the first question is answered by implication from what we can get into as answer to the second. That is, "truth" comes through experimental "action", rather than "action" embodying predetermined "truth".

In some situations, the Gospel reader, office-holder, minister or preacher tackles these two questions in a solo performance. In increasing numbers of contexts, the "work on the word" is done by the whole congregation, either with or without such an introductory exposition. In larger congregations, this "people's exposition" is done in smaller groups of participants. The questions they tackle usually include:

- What does this spark off as something we could do?
- What ways could we embody aspects or insights of this story?
- What attitudes are supported or suggested here?
- What possible projects could mirror or contain elements of this?

All these are ways of "Actualising the Text", which Louise Lawrence describes,[6] which is "reading the text in light of new circumstances", as Christopher Rowland puts it.[7]

This kind of "People's Bible Study", or "Practical Bible Study", or "Popular Bible Study" might well take some time, and is usually done on weekday evenings by small groups in members' homes, either before or after the passage is read on a Sunday in the worship setting. In some cases, the Gospel reading in a set lectionary is used.

---

[6] Louise Lawrence, "On a Cliff's Edge: Actualising Lk. 8.22-39", *Expository Times* 119.3, 2007, pp. 111-15.

[7] Cf. Christopher Rowland, "What Have We Here?", in *Mark: Gospel of Action*, pp. 3-8 (p. 5).

However, the expectation of Practice Interpretation is that hearers are disciples who intend to do something about the passage in their own lives, so that more than a single hearing is required. The study leads naturally to the question: "What shall we do in the light of this?", which needs to be followed up in further meetings which would develop the insights or suggestions discerned, in terms of changed practice in community life, church project, personal discipleship or liturgical expression. In each case, the "fruit" which comes from the "seed" of the word (cf. Mark 4.14) needs time to go through the processes of growth and maturation – first the stalk, then the ear, then the full grain in the ear, then the fully ripe grain (4.28–29).

To listen to new Gospel "words" without giving any of them the chance to "sink in" and "die" and then "bring forth fruit" (John 12.24) is the height of irresponsibility, and simply leads to the waste and unfruitfulness of the Gospel passages and of the Gospel itself.

This use of Gospel for practice and projects has been documented well in records of the methods used in the base ecclesial communities of South America, South Africa and elsewhere.[8] There are many such base ecclesial communities in Western Europe which follow the method.

Nearer home, this kind of "work on the word" has been a feature of many small urban Christian communities[9]. Such communities form the Sheffield Inner City Ecumenical Mission, and some of their experience with embodying and activating Gospel stories and concerns have been recorded.[10]

2. The Storm–Stilling Story

The story of the stilling of the storm by Jesus is found in the Gospel of Mark, 4.35–5.1. In a literal translation,[11] the passage reads:

> That same day, when it became evening, he said to them,
> "Let us cross over to the other side of the lake".

---

[8] Cf. Christopher Rowland and Jonathan Roberts, *The Bible for Sinners: Interpretation in the Present Times*, London: SPCK, 2008, pp. 45-60.

[9] See Christopher Rowland and John Vincent, eds., *Gospel from the City, British Liberation Theology*, vol. II, Sheffield: Urban Theology Unit, 1997; John Vincent, ed., *Faithfulness in the City*, Hawarden: Monad Press, 2003; Laurie Green, *Urban Ministry and the Kingdom of God*, London: SPCK, 2003.

[10] In John Vincent, *Hope from the City*, Peterborough: Epworth, 2000.

[11] This translation is by the writer, based on a study of the Greek text, plus comparison with various contemporary translations.

So they left the crowd where they were, and took him with them
in the boat, just where he had been sitting.
And there were other boats which also travelled with him.
A heavy wind-storm came on, and the waves broke over the boat,
so that the boat was being flooded.
Now he was in the stern of the boat, asleep on a cushion.
They woke him up, and said, "Master, we are being drowned.
Don't you care?"
He stood up, rebuked the wind, and addressed the sea:
"Hush! Be still!"
The wind dropped, and a great calm descended.
He said to them, "Why are you such cowards? Have you even now
no faith?"
They were filled with great fear, and said to one another,
"Who then can this man be, that even the wind and the sea obey
him?"

David Blatherwick describes many of the aspects of the story which
have given rise to varied interpretations. David's "take" on the story
emerges. He sees the story as a testing of the disciples, like Jesus' testing
in the temptation. He writes:

> 4.25–5.1 is not so much about Jesus stilling a storm as about his dis-
> ciples failing to cope with one, and his action is not so much a
> demonstration of his power as a necessary intervention if he and his
> disciples are not to drown.[12]

The disciples' question, "Who then is this?"

> … is not to be understood as in almost all biblical exegesis, in terms
> of Jesus' unique status in relation to God, but in terms of his rela-
> tionship to those who wield power in the world.[13]

One problem obviously relates to the historicity of the story. As David Blatherwick shows, stories of storm-stilling miracles and hero-
stories were not unknown in ancient literature, although only present
in Judaistic traditions with Yahweh as the heroic agent. Similarly, disciples as failing co-workers or divine-figure companions are not unknown.
So far as Mark is concerned, the story has been seen as a Markan
"divine man" construction[14], designed to commend Jesus to a Gentile
audience as a comparable wonder-worker to classic Greek heroes. On

---

[12] David Blatherwick, p. 26.

[13] David Blatherwick, p. 26.

[14] Paul J. Achtermeier, "The Origin and Function of the pre-Markan Miracle *Cate-
nae*", *Journal of Biblical Literature* 91 (1972), pp. 198-221.

this view, the whole of chs. 1 to 8 are an "aretalogy"[15] – a story of a god acting on earth, leading to the question to the disciples, "Who do you think this man is?", which the Judaistic disciples answer, "the, or a, Judaistic Anointed One" (Mark 8.29). Jesus in fact retorts by continuing the more Gentile-relevant title "son of humanity" (Mark 8.31), which is a Markan theme.[16]

The question of historicity might well be our first problem with the passage. It is the issue of whether or not the story is a more or less accurate record of an incident which actually happened. David Blatherwick concludes: "I doubt if Mark believed that the incident he describes ever happened." John Davies sees the story as being about how disciples are called for the sake of the new Kingdom of God on earth to be "at the storm centre" where demons act as supernatural powers, and being at the storm centre, "not because we are separated from God, but because we are with Christ". Andrew Parker observes that for the world in general, "nature miracles" are out of the question, but the phenomenon of charismatic power-yielding is not – for which he sees historical possibilities, and this story as an example of the possible effects of charismatic power over others.[17]

Others of us leave the question of historicity totally aside. Our interest is in the present "life" of the story, which is not in practice determined by whether an historical incident, whatever that might have been, actually lies behind it.

3. "Takes" and "Takings" by Disciples Today

The original manuscripts of Mark had the narrative as one continuing whole. Verses and chapters were added later, so that our storm stilling story belongs between the parables of the Kingdom in Mark 4.1–34, and the healing of the demon-possessed man in 5.2–20. Our interpreters are almost evenly divided between those who see the storm stilling story as essentially a development of the parables verses which precede it, and those who see it as the lake journey leading to the "demoniac" confrontation which follows it.

John Davies, Leslie Francis and others see the storm-stilling as primarily related to the chapters and verses that precede it.

---

[15] Achtemeier, p. 199.

[16] Cf. Joel Marcus, "Son of Man as Son of Adam", Part II: Exegesis, *Revue Biblique* 110 (2003), pp. 370-86.

[17] Blatherwick, p. 26; Davies, p. 29; Parker, p. 33.

For Louise Lawrence, the focus is on getting across the lake to tackle mission opportunities at the end of it. For me, the journey is to "the other side", represented by a particularly threatening context in inner city Sheffield. Disciples, full of Kingdom goodies (4.1–34) try them out in an alien context, with mixed results. Leslie Francis sees the projected journey as calls "to openness, to adventure and to change".

"Takes" and "takings" can often be influenced by temperamental types and preferences, so Leslie Francis asks that "each preferred voice be set alongside three other distinctive voices to which equal revelatory authority needs to be given". Sensing prefers conservatism, Intuition suggests innovation, Feeling prefers mercy, Thinking goes for justice.[18] But all are needed.

Four particular elements in the story are taken up by us as being suggestive or useful for contemporary experience. They will be taken in turn. They are: The Storm, The Boat, The Disciples, and The Other Side.

The Storm

Neil Richardson asks, "What is the "killer" storm raging among us?" Climate change, global capitalism ("Pax Romana with the stench of death")? Even if "a church which, even in its unbelief, cries out to God will not be overcome", yet its members must battle against contemporary "killers".[19]

The storm points to consequences for Christian discipleship. John Davies says:

> When the servants of God are consciously seeking God's Kingdom in the world, the powers of darkness will converge; they will seek to claim the apparently mindless forces and powers in opposition. Our discipleship of Christ may well appear to make things worse.[20]

The Boat

Not many of us pick up the traditional Christian use of the boat as representing the Church. Chris Burdon, who in fact does follow this line, sees the boat community situation as a sign of confusion rather than salvation, in a sea of persecution and temptation – and a sleeping Lord (with Tertullian). The other two boat stories in Mark (6.47–52 and 8.14–21) also indicate both disciples' failure and also "harsh frustra-

---

[18] Leslie Francis, pp. 85-86.
[19] Neil Richardson, pp. 59, 62.
[20] John Davies, p. 31.

tion on the part of Jesus".[21] Moreover, a sleeping Jesus is no great mark of the Church; and there are also "other boats", other "churches" or followers not of Jesus and his twelve (or more) disciples.

However, Louise Lawrence sees the boat and its crew as a missional unit carrying its Kingdom freight as gift into "changing cultural waters". Ian Wallis has the boat as the church, with an apparently sleeping Lord, but then builds a material boat as part of a course on "The Art of Living", whose participants are later invited to board. The "Ship of Fools" is off!

The Disciples

One striking element in the expositions in this volume is the attention given to the record in the story that the disciples themselves are expected by Jesus to have been able on their own to deal with the great storm. David Blatherwick sees the passage as following Mark 4.1–31, with its emphasis on disciples being given Kingdom secrets (4.11), and comments:

> The disciples are scared (4.41a); they realise that Jesus means it when he speaks of the coming of God's Kingdom and that he wants them to become agents of change, ambassadors of mercy, the Kingdom's heralds (4.41b).[22]

John Davies sees the disciples drawn into Jesus' battles with the storm-centres of evil. Andrew Parker sees the disciples as being expected to mirror the hero's charism by being able themselves to still the storm "if they had had the right attitude".[23] Ian Wallis, in a previous piece, took this view.[24]

For Susan Miller, "the boat journey acts as a metaphor for discipleship", and "disciples" here and elsewhere "may include women", perhaps in the other boats. The women later replicate the male disciples' fear and yet clinging – though in reverse order. Neil Richardson sees "deep inconsistency in their discipleship".[25] They stay with Jesus, but act with "un-disciple-like behaviour".

The disciples complain to Jesus, "Don't you care that we are perishing?"

---

[21] Burdon, p. 42.

[22] Blatherwick, p. 17.

[23] Parker, p. 35.

[24] Ian Wallis, *The Faith of Jesus Christ in the Early Christian Traditions*, Cambridge: Cambridge: Cambridge University Press, 1995, pp. 36–41.

[25] Richardson, p. 56.

Alan Saxby sees this response in terms of "fight or flight". In the disciples' case, they are caught between "flight" and "fight". Today, says Alan:

> Although real physical danger can confront us at any time, for many of us the threats and anxieties that gnaw away at our sense of comfort, well-being, self-worth and happiness on a daily basis arise mainly from issues of relationship, position, status and recognition, from the anxieties of mounting bills and "making ends meet", or from the sheer uncertainty and ambiguity of much that is going on around us (frequently reinforced by our 24/7 news culture).[26]

We respond today by "energetic activity, alcohol and drug abuse, music, sport", or by taking it out on ourselves or others – the "demonic within". A healing might come from "the practice and experience of stillness."

The Other Side

Several of us use the boat journey as an image for the journey of Jesus and disciples over into hostile or suspicious Gentile territory, which the Church finds difficult. So Susan Miller, following Ched Myers. In their fear which leads to faith, the women of 16.8 reflect the disciples of 4.41. Louise Lawrence sees the whole enterprise of "pushing the boat out" as disciples being "purposefully called out from the familiarity of home not only to encounter another world but also to found a new people", initially in the ten Gentile towns, through the healed demoniac's testimony (Mark 5.20). Ian Wallis sees how courageous non-church people venture to church as a feared "other side", which in their case is the church!

4. A D.I.Y. for Practice Interpretation

Practice Interpretation is an invitation to all readers to join in the same activity as the writers of these essays. This last section therefore draws together some ways in which the reader can enter into the ongoing life of the storm stilling story today.

I suggest a five-point strategy. Not every method will be useful for every occasion, but each brings its own rewards.

1. Live Your Way into the Story

First, get the story into your system! Several ways of doing this are useful.

---

[26] Saxby, p. 93.

(1) Read the passage over, two or three times. Get the sequence of events clear. Use David Blatherwick's ten-point outline as a check (pp. 17f.).

(2) Tell the story to yourself – or, better, to someone else, in your own words. Significantly, almost all of us in these essays actually repeat the story, as a whole or decisive bits of it, in our own words. We are making the story our own. It's now "our story".

2. Act out the Story

In a group, get individuals or pairs to represent Jesus, the disciples, plus the storm and the boat if you wish! Follow the method of John Davies for acting out the story.[27]

1. Divide your group into four, representing

   - Jesus
   - The Disciples
   - Mark, the Author
   - Early Church Group

2. Get each group to study the passage, and to act their way into the character.

   - What are the interests of the character?
   - How do they view the boat?
   - How do they view the storm?

3. Then get a discussion going – Each group sends a delegate to the other groups

   - Jesus to disciples: You are the problem, because …
   - Disciples to Jesus: You are the problem, because …
   - Mark to early Church: You are the problem, because …
   - Early Church to Mark: You are the problem, because …
   - Jesus to Mark: Why do you tell this story?
   - Disciples to Mark: Why do you tell this story?
   - Mark to early Church: Why do you tell this story?
   - Early Church to Mark: Why do you tell this story?

4. Finally, each group concludes:

---

[27] This method is an adaptation for this passage of many examples in the writings of John D. Davies. See Davies and Vincent, *Mark at Work*, London: Bible Reading Fellowship, 1986, pp. 16-18; John Davies, *Only Say the Word*, Norwich: Canterbury Press, 2002, pp. 33-37.

- What it has learned.
- What it now needs to do.

3. Question the Story

Pick up any odd points. What seem to you to be issues arising? Ask yourself, or others if you can do it in a group, what the different bits of the story open up in terms of problems or insights or possibilities.

At this stage, consider David Blatherwick's "Two Basic Issues":[28]

1. Is it a miracle story, or a story about the behaviour of disciples?
2. Does it belong with the preceding passage on parables?

Then you could move on to David's eighteen questions in his Part 2: "Some More Important Questions".

By now you might have got your own "New Proposal" for interpreting the passage. Use David's "New Proposal" (Section 3, pp. 3–5) if you haven't got your own yet.

4. Take Your Context to the Story

Here, the methods of Liberation Theology and Contextual Bible Study are crucially relevant. In these methods, people make an analysis of their own context in terms of issues of equality, freedom and justice – and then learn from how people in a biblical time in a similar context dealt with similar issues.

In several volumes edited by Christopher Rowland and myself, examples are given of Liberation Theology in action in Britain.[29] The principle of giving priority to action and practice in relation to the experience of oppression and injustice is crucial to Liberation Theology. The question naturally follows, in terms of biblical exegesis, "Where are the interests of the victims of society being championed?" – and, by implication, championed by God.

Gerald West and Bongi Zengele give the method which they follow in working with small community groups. The method could apply to any groups of disciples who were sharing a common social situation and common problems and issues.

1. Retell the story in your own words in "buzz groups" of two. What is the text about?

---

[28] Blatherwick, p. 18.
[29] Christopher Rowland and John Vincent, eds., *British Liberation Theology*, 4 vols., Sheffield: Urban Theology Unit, 1995, 1997, 1999, 2001.

2. Who is sailing the boat, and what is Jesus doing in the boat?

3. When and why do the disciples wake Jesus?

4. What are they afraid of?

5. What are we who are living with this situation and these issues afraid of?

6. Is Jesus in "the boat" with us? If he is, is he asleep or awake?

7. If Jesus is still asleep, how do we wake him up?

8. If he is awake or if he were to waken, what would we want him to do?

9. What does this story challenge us to do?

This method is useful for any Christian group which meets together to do Bible study as part of their search for their own contextual community and personal responses to scripture.

5. Take Your Practice to the Text

Throughout this volume, we bring our present-day practice to the text. Christopher Rowland has written:

> How you live or act conditions the way in which you understand. In other words, the practice of the life of discipleship and the context in which that discipleship takes place throw up understandings of text which would only with difficulty have emerged in the calm reflection of academy or church.[30]

For this, several contributors might be useful. Chris Burdon describes the ways in which a small parish group imagined themselves into the story, particularly identifying themselves with the disciples in the boat.

Louise Lawrence tells of insights from Cornish fishermen and small village communities arising in small rural study groups. Leslie Francis shows how Temperament Analysis assists us to encounter the story. Alan Saxby sees the story from his experience with people under stress. Gerald West and Bongi Zengele are demanding action for HIV and Aids victims, Ian Wallis that the sleeping Jesus should live in Houghton-le-Spring, I myself that he be in inner city Sheffield.

Our witness is that it is perfectly legitimate to bring to the story experiences and even conclusions and perspectives that derive not at all

---

[30] Christopher Rowland, "Practical Exegesis in Context", *Bible and Practice*, ed. Christopher Rowland and John Vincent, British Liberation Theology, 4; Sheffield: Urban Theology Unit, 2001, pp. 10-26 (p. 12).

from the Gospel context, but from contemporary engagement to which various of us have felt dawn or impelled as implications of our own "calls" as disciples. Thus, the "call" has come to individuals which has landed them in particular locations which then are the "sites" in which they expect that Gospel-like further calls and happenings will take place. This is true for many of us. The calls to ordained ministry (eight of us!) are in the end only doorways which open up to a variety of specific "calls", often to mutually contradictory tasks and situations, and take us to specific locations, with specific institutions, and with particular people. These in turn determine the places and people we listen to, are influenced by, do Bible study with, seek to address, and develop projects with.

No "hearer" is context-free. Every hearer operates within a context and seeks both to hear the Gospel there, and to speak it there. Each reader is invited to take her/himself, each with their own context, call and commitments, to the story, as one more unique "site" for its "coming to life" yet one more time again.

6. Expect Some Practice from the Story

Practice emerges – the earlier morning "Be Still" worship service at Barnsley, the mission on Spital Hill in Sheffield, the boat to carry discipleship trainees in Houghton-le-Spring, the Devon fishermen raising whether Church is Fishing Trawler or Passenger Ferry, the mission with and of HIV and AIDS in KwaZulu Natal, the naming and confrontation of evil powers in apartheid South Africa, the discovery and affirmation of alternative Gospel Communities in Chris Burdon, the welcome to women passengers and crew in Susan Miller, the identification of secular messianic charismatic operators in Andrew Parker, the support and understanding for "unbelieving believers" in Neil Richardson, the SIFT Bible study method as a programme for discipleship development in Leslie Francis.

Partly, what practice the story dictates or suggests will depend upon who the group is which is going to the text, and what their commitments are. Disciples today in this book often see themselves as being driven to be like frightened disciples in a boat, buffeted by great storms, carrying an apparently sleeping Jesus, but knowing that they have to ride out the storm in order to get Jesus to "the other side", where his work is sorely needed. So the readings of John Davies, Chris Burdon, Louise Lawrence, John Vincent and Gerald West/Bongi Zengele.

Thus, a natural question to a reader and/or her/his community would have to be: What is the great storm you know you have to deal with? And what is the future mission of Jesus which is only possible if you get him through the storm to the other side, where he can deal with it?

Another question might be: What's with you and your people in your context that you don't feel you are in a storm? Has Jesus lulled you all to sleep? Is there no storm anywhere that you might be being called to get yourselves into the middle of?

So, where are you as a disciple, and you and your friends as a disciple community, up to in all this? And where could you be? Or where should you be?

2

Some Questions and a Proposal

DAVID BLATHERWICK

1. The Outline of Mark 4.35–5.1 and Two Basic Issues

Mark's story of Jesus stilling a storm on the lake has this simple outline:

1. Jesus invites his disciples to go to the other side (4.35). He does not define the destination more precisely and gives the invitation in the evening of the day he sat in a boat on the lake teaching only in parables (cf. 4.1–34).
2. The disciples accept his invitation, leaving the crowd behind, and take him with them in the boat. There are other boats with them (4.36).
3. A horrendous storm breaks and very soon the boat is near sinking (4.37).
4. Jesus is fast asleep in the stern, on the cushion (4.38a).
5. The disciples react badly (4.38b, c).
6. Jesus acts immediately to stop the storm and save everyone's life (4.39a).
7. The wind dies down and the lake is eerily calm (4.39b).
8. Jesus asks the disciples why they reacted badly (4.40).
9. The disciples are scared (4.41a); they realise that Jesus means it when he speaks of the coming of God's kingdom and that he wants them to become agents of change, ambassadors of mercy, the kingdom's heralds (4.41b).

10.   They arrive on the other side of the lake, in the country of the Gerasenes – and any mystery surrounding their precise destination disappears (5.1).[1]

Two basic issues arise:

1.   Most people see it simply as a rescue, or nature, miracle story. Some see that it is not just such a story, but one that also highlights the disciples' inability to cope with the storm. Others think Mark puts the emphasis on the disciples rather than Jesus. We shall need to decide where we stand on this issue as we proceed.[2]

2.   Related to this, we shall need to decide what significance Mark attaches to his placing of the story next to the parable teaching of 4.1–34 – and, more specifically, on the evening of the same day. Matthew places it after the healings of Mark 1.20–38 and some time before Jesus elects the Twelve (8.18–27). Luke places it after the parable of the sower, but not the two warning parables,[3] and on another day (8.22–26).[4]

2. Some More Important Questions

Other questions that may arise as we read the story include these:

1.   Why set out "in the evening"? It was estimated that, in normal circumstances, a boat could cross the lake in two to three hours.[5] It takes the disciples longer in 6.45–52, because they are rowing into a headwind. So they should reach "the other side" in darkness, at about 8 or 9 p.m.

---

[1] The chapter divisions that were introduced into our Bible in the Middle Ages are not always a reliable guide as to where one story or section ends and another begins.

[2] Much of the scholarly discussion around Mark 4.35–5.1 relates to its redaction. Did Mark alter a story that presented Jesus as a miracle-worker to develop a discipleship theme? If so, what did he add? There is, however, no end to the conjectures we can make about the pre-Markan story and no way of knowing which of them, if any, is right. For present purposes, we shall concentrate on the text as it stands.

[3] The parables of the seed growing secretly and the mustard are usually described as parables of growth and assumed to give positive messages about the coming of the kingdom. But Mark places them after a warning to watch what we hear, "for to those who have, more will be given; and from those who have nothing, even what they have will be taken away" (4.24-25).

[4] Most commentaries and many translations encourage us to see 4.35–5.1 in relation to what follows it rather than what precedes it. But the links with 4.1-34 are strong and, apart from the fact that the boat's arrival on the other shore brings Jesus to the scene of 5.2-20, it has few clear links with what follows.

[5] This was the view of a third-century philosopher quoted by Macarius Magnes, in *Apokritos* 3.6-19, 26.

2. Who is in charge of the boat – Jesus or the disciples?
3. What is the significance of the other boats?
4. Are they hit by a squall, a gale or a whirlwind (*lailaps*)? Several commentators refer to sudden storms that occur on the lake and assume that Mark has one of those in mind. But *lailaps* usually means a whirlwind or hurricane (e.g. Homer, *Iliad* 17.4) and Mark refers to a whirlwind or hurricane "of great wind". (The author of *Testament of Naphtali* 6.4 uses a similar phrase with reference to the storm that sweeps Jacob from the helm of his boat, breaks the boat up and scatters his sons across the seas.)[6]
5. How quickly does the boat fill?
6. What is the significance of Jesus' position "in the stern, on the cushion"? (Why do Matthew and Luke both omit that detail?)
7. Why are the disciples upset because he is asleep? Why shouldn't he be?
8. Does Jesus stop the storm as soon as he wakes to demonstrate his supernatural powers or because, if he doesn't, they will all drown?
9. Why is Jesus so angry with his disciples afterwards (4.40)?
10. What does Mark mean by *deilos*? The lexicons say it means "cowardly, timid". Many translators and commentators say it means "frightened, terrified" (cf. the verb in John 14.27). Jesus might think it reasonable for the landlubbers among the disciples to have been frightened – but not the fishermen who should have known what to do! Yet even frightened people can display courage in the face of danger.[7]
11. What sort of faith does Jesus look for? Do we assume that Jesus saw his sleep as an expression of his confidence in God (cf. Pss 3.5–6; 4.8) and had expected his disciples to be equally confident? Do we assume that he thought he had given them all the evidence they needed for them to know they only had to ask him for help and they would have been safe (cf. Pss 35.22–23; 44.23, 26)? Or did he see faith as loyalty or faithfulness?[8] Could they not just do the job they had been entrusted with, whatever the dangers or risks, and show determination in seeking to reach their goal?

---

[6] *Testament of Naphtali* 6 probably predates Mark's Gospel, but dating it is difficult.

[7] According to Deut 20.8, there is no room for anyone who is cowardly or afraid in Yahweh's army (LXX: *ho phoboumenos kai deilos tē kardia*; cf. also Judg 7.3).

[8] In Rev 21.8, the cowardly and faithless head the list of those who will be consigned to "the lake that burns with fire and sulphur, which is the second death".

12. Did Mark and/or Jesus see the storm as a demon? Mark uses the same words, *epitiman* and *phimoun*, in 1.25, when Jesus commands and silences a demon. *epitiman* is used in the Septuagint version of Zechariah 3.2, where Yahweh commands Satan to leave Jerusalem alone, and Jude 9, where the archangel Michael overcomes Satan in a battle over Moses' remains. The Septuagint translators also use *epitiman* and the noun *epitimēsis* in a number of passages where Yahweh commands the unruly elements and brings them back under his control (e.g. Pss 18.13–15; 104.5–7; 106.9–10). Is Mark using the verb with texts like these in mind? Does he also see a command to silence as an exorcistic device, not just a command to silence, as some scholars claim?

13. Is the disciples' "great fear" a reaction to the miracle (i.e. awe) or a reaction to Jesus' criticism? Might we be less inclined to see it as awe, if we did not see *deilos* in 4.40 as "frightened, terrified"? The words *phobos* and *phobeisthai* can refer to feelings of awe or wonder, just as their English equivalents can, but usually denote simple fear or terror. Do the disciples sense Jesus' anger and realise that there will be other, much severer, tests of their courage and faith in the future?

14. Who else has authority to command the wind and the sea and they obey him? Yahweh has. Greek and Roman deities have.[9] So do heroes like Hercules,[10] magicians like Pythagoras[11] and kings or generals like Xerxes, Alexander the Great, Pompey and the Caesars.[12]

---

[9] In his *Odes* Horace refers to Venus and Aeolus (1.3), Neptune (1.5), the twins Castor and Pollux (1.3; 1.12; 3.29), Bacchus (2.19) and Fortuna (1.7; 1.35). Other deities who were thought to protect people at sea who were popular at that time include Isis (Apuleius, *The Golden Ass* 11.11-24; Pausanias, *Travels* 2.2.3; Juvenal, *Satires* 12) Asclepius (Pausanias, *Travels* 2.2.3; 2.10.2) and Serapis (Tacitus, *Histories* 4.84; Aelius Aristides, *Oratio* 45.29).

[10] Hercules has power over the elements (e.g. Horace, *Odes* 1.3; 1.12; Epictetus, *Dissertations* 3.26.32). So does Orpheus (e.g. Horace, *Odes* 1.12; Diodorus Siculus, *Library* 4.43.1-2; 4.48.5-6).

[11] Porphyry lists some of Pythagoras's powers in his *Life of Pythagoras* 29 and names Empedocles as one of the disciples with whom he shared his secrets (cf. Iamblichus, *Life* 28). Diogenes Laertius lists some of the claims Empedocles made for himself (*Lives of Eminent Philosophers* 8.59). Apollonius of Tyana was also thought to have power over the sea (cf. Philostratus, *Life of Apollonius* 4.13-15).

[12] Xerxes: Herodotus, *Histories* 7.33-36; 8.116-120; Juvenal, *Satires* 10.174-188; Lucretius, *On the Nature of the Universe* 1029-1034; Alexander: Plutarch, *Alexander* 17; Josephus, *Antiquities* 2.347-348): Pompey: Cicero, *On the Command* 16; Plutarch, *Pompey* 50; Petronius, *Satyricon* 123; Augustus: Ovid, *Metamorphoses* 15.745-870; Inscriptions at Halicarnassus and Myra in Lycia; cf. also Horace, *Odes* 1.2. Claudius: Seneca, *Octavia* 34-56; Nero: *ibid.* 472-491. In Jewish tradition, Moses also makes the sea obey him (Exod

15. Does the story end with the simple statement that they reach "the other side" or with the clarification that they have now reached "the country of the Gerasenes"? That is, how important is it for our understanding of the story to recognise that Jesus was taking the disciples into unknown, probably Gentile territory and that they might have been in two minds about what they were doing? Whether they reach the country of the Gerasenes or that of the Gadarenes is unimportant. Gerasa and Gadara were two cities on the other side of the lake, founded or resettled after Alexander the Great's conquest of the Middle East by people who were loyal to him and part of a federation of Greek cities known as the Decapolis (the Ten Cities). Both were a good way from the lake.[13]

16. Is it helpful to see 4.35–5.43 as a unity – even as a pre-Markan unit?

17. Are there echoes of other stories, or familiar biblical passages, in Mark's text? We have already noted that some people think Jesus' sleep in the storm resembles that of the Psalmist in Pss 4.8 and 3.5–6, that the disciples' action in waking him is like that of the Psalmist in waking Yahweh in Pss 35.22–23 and 44.23, 26 or that Jesus' rebuke to the wind is like that of Yahweh to the elements in Pss 18.13–15, 104.5–7 and 106.9–10. Some think the sequence of events in Mark 4.38–5.1 is similar to that in Ps 107.28–30, where the sailors cry out in their distress, Yahweh hears them, stills the storm and brings them safely home. Some point to the verbal echoes of Jonah 1 in Mark 4.35–5.1 and try to find a thematic link between the two. Finally, there are some who wonder whether Mark wanted his readers to see a link between this story and that of Julius Caesar trying to sail from Apollonia to Brundisium in a small boat and rough seas during his war with Pompey.[14] Jesus reaches his destination, Caesar turns back!

18. Should we read the story as fact, supposed fact or fiction? Most people assume that it is an account of something that really happened in the course of Jesus' ministry, or that Mark

---

14.21; Philo, *Life of Moses* I.155-157), Elijah and Elisha stop the Jordan in its tracks (2 Kgs 2.8, 14) and Yahweh gives David authority over the sea and the rivers (Ps 89.25).

[13] Both "Gerasenes" and "Gadarenes" have good manuscript support and it is difficult to choose between them. Gadara was about 7 miles from the lakeside and Gerasa about 30. Neither reading sits easily with 5.14. The reading "Gergesenes" has less support and "Gergustenes" very little.

[14] The story is in Ammianus, *History* 16.10.3; Appian, *Civil War* 2.8.4; Cassius Dio, *Roman History* 41.46; Lucan, *Civil War* 560-702; Plutarch, *Caesar* 38; Suetonius, *Caesar* 58.

thought happened, which may have been embellished to highlight certain points or teach certain lessons. But there are some who see it as a story that was made up to present Jesus in a certain light and passed off as fact. Rudolf Bultmann describes it as an alien miracle story, based on the Jewish legend which also forms the basis for the stories in Jonah 1 and *y. Berakhot* 9.13b, that has been applied to Jesus.[15] David F. Strauss says it is woven out of strands drawn from various Psalms.[16] Rudolf Pesch sees the original miracle story as a free rendering of Jonah 1, with added colour taken from Ps 107.23–32 and the tradition of Jesus as exorcist and teacher.[17] Roger Aus thinks the author has drawn on a wide range of Jonah traditions to create the story, but probably also expects readers to see a contrast between Jesus who does make the wind do his bidding and Caesar who does not.[18]

3. A New Proposal

I doubt if scholars until now have taken sufficient account of some remarkable features of Mark's text. The wind that strikes the boat is *lailaps megalē anemou*; not a squall or gale, but a whirlwind or hurricane of immense power. Its immediate effect is that the boat is awash and near sinking. The disciples stare death in the face, but Jesus is asleep in the stern of the boat, on the cushion. They do not wake him up to alert him to the danger or ask him to help but to accuse him of lack of concern or dereliction of duty. Jesus then stills the storm and accuses them of cowardice and lack of faith. They are stunned and quite unable to respond to his attack.

We are so wedded to the realistic interpretation of Mark's story that we do not see the storm as anything abnormal or recognise that the disciples' boat is going down within minutes of it breaking. It is like the storm sent by Poseidon in Homer, *Odyssey* 5.282–493 that destroys Odysseus's boat almost as soon as it strikes and leaves him to fight for his life, the storm in *Testament of Naphtali* 6.4 (*lailaps anemou megas*) that sweeps Jacob overboard and drives his sons helplessly before it, or the storms of Jonah 1, Ps 107.23–32 and Virgil, *Aeneid* 1.81–142.

---

[15] Rudolf Bultmann, *The History of the Synoptic Tradition*, Oxford: Blackwell, 1963, pp. 234-35.

[16] David F. Strauss, *The Life of Jesus Critically Examined*, Philadelphia: Fortress, 1972, p. 498.

[17] Rudolph Pesch, *Das Markusevangelium*, 2 vols., Freiburg/Basle: Herder, 1976/78, pp. 267-81.

[18] Roger David Aus, *The Stilling of the Storm*, Binghamton/New York: Global Publications, 2000, pp. 1-87.

Nor do we register the awkwardness of Jesus' position in the boat. The stern is the place from which the helmsman operates. Jesus would be very much in the way on the stern deck or just in front of it. Shelley Wachsmann suggests that he was under the deck (taking *en*, in, literally), not on it.[19] But surely he would be in the way there too. A few brave souls argue that Jesus was the helmsman. Herman Waetjen thinks he had fallen asleep, let his hand slip from the steering oar and left the disciples on their own. When they wake him up and remind him of his duties, he says they should have taken responsibility, grabbed the oar and fought the storm. They need to appropriate and use the authority he is sharing with them, not leave him to solve all their problems.[20]

Some of Mark's readers would, of course, have been familiar with the motif of the sleeping helmsman – or that of the sleeping commander or head of state. Odysseus falls asleep at the helm in calm seas within sight of home (Homer, *Odyssey* 10.17–55). Aeneas's helmsman, Palinurus, goes to sleep and falls overboard in similar conditions (Virgil, *Aeneid* 5.835–871). Mithridates, the Parthian king, dreams he is at the helm of a boat, nearing home, but wakes to find himself surrounded (Plutarch, *Pompey* 32; cf. also Cicero, *On Duties* 1.22.77; Horace, *Odes* 2.13). Of course, Mithridates is a king and the leader of an army, not a helmsman, but the message holds good for leaders of armies and nations. No one responsible for other people's welfare or safety is allowed to sleep when danger threatens or there is no one else to put in charge. Mercury chides Aeneas for sleeping in the stern of his ship when he and his companions are in danger (Virgil, *Aeneid* 4.554–570; but Aeneas is awake for most of the night in 8.13–30, as he prepares for battle). Agamemnon is similarly chided for sleeping while his armies are in disarray (Homer, *Iliad* 2.25–40). Jason cannot sleep because he is responsible for so many people's lives (Apollonius of Rhodes, *The Voyage of Argo* 2.619–637). Oedipus assures the priest who informs him of Thebes's plight that he is not asleep (Sophocles, *Oedipus the King* 64–65). Xenophon realises he cannot sleep when he and his fellow soldiers are in imminent danger in Persia (*The Persian Expedition* 1.3.11; 3.1.11–18). Vincent Taylor sees the parallels between Mark 4.38 and *Aeneid* 4.554–570 as quite as impressive as any found in the Hebrew Bible or

---

[19] Shelley Wachsmann, *The Sea of Galilee Boat*, Cambridge, Mass.: Perseus, 2000, pp. 326–28. Wachsmann says a position on top of the stern deck would be rather precarious but a position under it would be sheltered and out of the way. He says the cushion that Mark mentions could be the large ballast sack that some boats in the region still carry.

[20] Herman C. Waetjen, *A Reordering of Power*, Minneapolis: Fortress Press, 1989, p. 112.

rabbinic texts, but cannot believe that Mark had read his Virgil.[21] But I am not suggesting that Mark has borrowed from that or any other earlier text, only that there is a shared assumption about the responsibility of people in leadership positions or positions of trust.

Most of Mark's readers would have also understood the use of ships, voyages, storms, reefs and shipwrecks as metaphors for life and its vicissitudes – for the sudden changes of fortune or hostile attacks that throw us off balance, the onslaughts of fierce emotion that threaten to drive our boat off course or capsize it and the crises that arise in the life of a city or state as a result of enemy invasion, weak or confused leadership or internal unrest.[22]

Mark 3.13–4.34 leads us to expect something more akin to the temptation story in 1.12–13 than the rescue miracle story most scholars see here. Jesus has selected the Twelve and they have become aware of the gulfs between him and his opponents and him and his family. They have seen him distance himself from the people on the shore who have come to hear him and heard him speak to them in parables only – but he has shared their meaning with them and a few others. The scene is set for an experience of testing comparable to that which Jesus underwent after his baptism and call. Like him, the disciples need to grasp what their call entails. He has told them, in his explanation of the sower parable, that they will face trials and may be found wanting. (He has also told them that they must be prepared for the long haul. It is tempting to see 4.35–5.1 as dramatising the first challenge and 6.45–52 as dramatising the second.) But those who are steadfast will produce a rich harvest. At this point, they leave the crowd – or most of it[23] – behind to go with him.

John Chrysostom suggests that Jesus goes to sleep so that his disciples will be on their own when the storm breaks, experience its full force for themselves and learn to turn to him for help (*Homilies on Matthew* 28). In Mark, Jesus' questions about the disciples' lack of courage and faith seem to suggest something different – that, if they had faced up to the storm and tried to outwit it, they would have been helped, as Jesus was helped in 1.13, or Shadrach, Meshach and Abednego were helped

---

[21] Vincent Taylor, *The Gospel according to St Mark*, London: Macmillan, 1957 (reprint of 1952 edition), p. 273.

[22] Hans-Josef Klauck, *Allegorie und Allegorese in synoptischen Gleichnistexten*, Münster: Aschendorf, 1978, pp. 340–45. Most of the examples Klauck gathers here are Greek or Roman. Judaism provides a good example in *Testament of Napthtali* 6. There Israel's history is presented as a voyage that Jacob and his sons undertake, her troubles are presented as a storm that sinks the ship and scatters them over the seas and her hope is in some way related to Levi's prayer and symbolised in the rejoicing at Jacob's return.

[23] Jesus has more than just the Twelve round him in 4.10-20, and presumably 4.34. The presence of the other boats in 4.36 suggests that a similarly enlarged group of disciples sails to the other side with him.

in Dan 3.24–30 and Daniel helped in Dan 6.16–28. Elsewhere in the gospel, faith is presented as a determination to overcome obstacles, a refusal to take No for an answer, a readiness to meet God half way (2.1–12; 5.21–43; 9.14–29; 10.46–52; 11.22–24; cf. 1.14–15).[24]

The disciples' response to the storm is very different from that of Odysseus to the storm that sinks his ship and leaves him to drown (Homer, *Odyssey* 5.568–618). Io and Athene help him, because he does not give up hope but fights for his life. It is also different from that of the Argonauts to clashing rocks that threaten to smash their boat and a towering wave that threatens to swamp it. Athene sees their bravery and nudges their boat out of the way of another wave and lets them go on (Apollonius of Rhodes, *The Voyage of Argo* 2.568–618). Shadrach, Meshach and Abednego do not fear death as they reply to Nebuchadnezzar (Dan 3.16–18) nor does Daniel as he defies Darius (Dan 6.1–15). If Yahweh will save them, fine. If not, that is fine too. What they will not do is deny their faith or be disloyal to their God. Yahweh helps them because they are brave – and maybe because they do not beg him to protect them or tell them what to do.

In the second-century *Shepherd of Hermas*, Hermas learns what it means to be a Christian through a number of visions. In the fourth he learns about persecution and how to meet it. He is told not to be double-minded and is wondering what that means when he sees a large cloud of dust and a monster coming towards him, threatening to destroy him. Trembling with fear, he starts to pray, but remembers that he must not be double-minded. He then walks boldly towards the monster, daring it to do its worst. It stops, lies down on the ground and lets him pass (*Visions* 4.1.1–9).[25]

If we see in Mark's story a similar test of the disciples' faith and courage, and one that is parallel to Jesus' experience of testing, it is clearly one they fail. 4.35–5.1 is not so much about Jesus stilling a storm as about his disciples failing to cope with one, and his action is not so

---

[24] The picture of Jesus asleep at the helm and the disciples having to take responsibility for completing the voyage to which he called them is, of course, an apt image for the situation that arises when Jesus is killed. Then the disciples have to accept responsibility for continuing his mission. Suetonius says that, shortly before his death, Nero dreamt that he was at the helm of a boat and the tiller was snatched away from him (*Nero* 46).

[25] For the concept of double-mindedness, cf. James 1.5-8. It is difficult for most of us to accept that, in some circumstances, it is wrong to pray, because we have been taught otherwise. But in Exod 14.15-18 Yahweh criticises Moses for crying out to him when he knows what he should do Yahweh will take care of the Egyptians, but the rest is up to him! In *Mekhilta* II, 222-223 he says in effect, "You have the sea in front of you and the Egyptian army behind you – and all you can do is pray!"

much a demonstration of his power as a necessary intervention if he and his disciples are not to drown.[26]

Running through the conversation in 4.38–40 is the question "Who is in charge of the boat?" Clearly the disciples think Jesus is, just as we tend to think God is in our lives. Jesus says they are.

The significance of the disciples' wondering question, "Who then is this…?" is therefore not that they are surprised that Jesus should possess powers that belong only to God, but that he actually has powers that men like Xerxes, Alexander, Pompey and the Caesars claim to have. Their question is not to be understood, as it is in almost all biblical exegesis, in terms of Jesus' unique status in relation to God, but in terms of his relationship to those who wield power in the world. He is the one to whom God gives all authority in heaven and earth,[27] who sends them into the world as his ambassadors (cf. Matt 28.18–20), who will come on the clouds to inaugurate God's reign (1.14–15; 9.1; 13.24–27; 14.61–62) but is now calling them to work with him, for whom they must be strong and resourceful and to whom they must be true.

I doubt if Mark believed the incident he describes ever happened. 4.35–5.1 has all the hallmarks of a fable – a story like those in Daniel 3 and 6, *Shepherd of Hermas, Vision* 4 and *Testament of Naphtali* 6 that conveys an important truth, inviting readers or hearers to look again at things they thought they understood, but see them with new eyes. It invites believers to look again at the nature of Christian discipleship and ask if they are strong enough and determined enough to stay the course. Matthew and Luke both seem to assume that the story is true – that it is an account of a miracle that Jesus performed. The dominance of Matthew's Gospel over Mark's in biblical exegesis until the 19th century means that we still tend to see Mark's story through Matthew's eyes – but tend to carry over into our reading of Matthew features of Mark's story (especially the stern and the cushion) that Matthew carefully omitted because they gave a picture of Jesus and a concept of discipleship that he didn't want to perpetuate.

---

[26] In the story of the Sorcerer's Apprentice, the sorcerer acts promptly to stop his house being flooded, not to display his superior skills (Lucian of Samosata, *Lover of Lies* 34-36).

[27] Cf. Horace, *Odes* 1.12, where Augustus is portrayed as Saturn's lieutenant. Saturn can now look after heaven and leave his lieutenant to spread justice efficiently throughout the world.

3

At the Storm Centre

JOHN D. DAVIES

Early in 2008, there was an extraordinary image on British TV News. An ordinary train was trundling along the railway line near Dawlish, and was completely swamped by a huge wave which crashed over the sea-wall. To us as spectators, it was an amazing sight. But for the passengers, it must have been terrifying. In other places along the south coast that day, the roads in one direction were full of frightened people trying to get away; and in the opposite direction, there were inquisitive people wanting to get closer to watch the spectacle.

What is your experience of storms? Have you been right in the middle, trying to find something to hold on to? Or, have you been a spectator, or a listener to someone else's story of a storm?

At the beginning of his ministry, Jesus calls people to follow him. "Come with me", he says. "I have a job for you. You are going to be catching people, influencing people, getting them into a community. You will be joining the movement of my kingdom."

Then what? Conflicts with demons, conflicts with religious authorities, conflicts even with his own family. "'Kingdom' you promised us", the followers might well say; "What 'kingdom'? All we can see is trouble and more trouble." So he tells them the parables of sowing and of secret growth. It's not going to be a straightforward swoop into power. For a lot of the time, the seed will appear to be wasted. There will be a harvest, but you will have to wait for it. You will have to cope with the setbacks. If this was not a world in which things go wrong, there would be no need of a Messiah, no need of a programme of salvation, no need of a coming kingdom.

So Jesus prepares his followers to meet trouble, in a world oppressed by demons and disasters. And so to the next act, a storm at sea.

Up till now, the only people to recognise something of the authority of Jesus are a few fishermen and their cronies; not the religious authorities; not the family. But demons see who he is, before any people (Mark 1.25). He is a threat to them. They are the powers of destruction, the agents of evil, which invade God's territory and dominate God's children. Right at the beginning of the story, there is this recognition. And here is a second instalment. The storm is not just a meteorological phenomenon; it is a symbol of the destructiveness of the powers of darkness. And it is in this character that Jesus meets it. He recognises it as a conscious spiritual power; he addresses it. He exorcises it with the command "be muzzled" – in the same terms that he had used to the demon in the synagogue. He shows that he can master it. It slinks off, leaving the scene as a scene of the peace of God's kingdom.

We are told of the terror of those who were at the heart of the storm, who experienced its sudden threat and destructiveness. But as well as Jesus and the disciples, we can recognise a third party, those on shore, spectators, relatives; they would be helpless, fascinated, worried. What about Peter's wife, Zebedee's family? "Stupid – if you hadn't gone and got hooked onto that Jesus, you could be safe at home in your beds." "Aren't you supposed to be fishermen? You should have known better than to have gone out when a storm was brewing!" Or, perhaps, they were not aware of it at all, until later.

The sea is terrifying. The storms on Galilee do not figure in a long-range weather-forecast; they are not generated far off in the distant ocean. They are sudden, local, unpredictable. The storm catches the Master asleep. So he treats it as a demon. Does this mean that we should interpret every tsunami or tornado as a supernatural event, not as the natural working-out of normal processes? We are not obliged to accept the language of "demons" as an essential of faith – we can live with the message of John's Gospel, for instance, without bothering about such language. But the "demons" do stand for something which many of us have found to be valid; they represent the power of evil, of hostility to God, which is bigger than life, going beyond the malice of the individual human motive. So, in this story the demon is specific. Because Christ is on the scene, it claims the mechanism of the storm as an instrument in an attempt to destroy him at this early stage of his ministry.

The disciples are there, in the storm, for only one reason: because Jesus has called them. He does not guarantee them good weather; but he is with them when the weather gets terrible. He does not create a protected zone around himself, where demons cannot approach; but he is able to be a powerful companion, when the demons do show what they are made of. They discover that he is Emmanuel, God with us. This is the final point that Mark is making in his telling of the story.

But the boat of Christ and his immediate followers is not the only boat on the water. There are others, for whatever reason. Perhaps they have thought that it would be convenient for a group of boats to go together if they were crossing to a new territory and avoiding the land-based check-points of the imperial system. The presence of Christ has affected them. They also have been caught up in the storm.

If we respond to the call to follow Jesus, we may well find ourselves in a scene of struggle, where the forces against us are much greater than the malice of individual bad people. We find ourselves in a scene where the blame for cruelty and disorder goes far beyond the individuals who seem to deserve the blame. "We wrestle not against flesh and blood but against cosmic powers, against the authorities and potentates of this dark world, against the superhuman forces of evil in the heavens" (Eph 6.12). We may find ourselves at a storm-centre, not because we are separated from God but because we are with Christ. We may feel deserted, derelict, let down. And we may well cry out in agony and disbelief, to a God whom we think will not be able to hear us, "We are perishing!" We will claim the old words of the psalms; when the forces of evil are strong around us, we will feel that God is asleep. Anyone who has been caught up in the mass ideologies of the twentieth century in the West, of Nazism, of Stalinism, of apartheid, will recognise this. We will come to realise that Christ is typically known, not in the Sabbath rest by Galilee but in the whirling wind's tempestuous shocks of that same Galilee. It is in that same Galilee that the risen Christ tells us that we will find him.

This storm-story is a first instalment of the ultimate battle. Jesus is threatened with the death of himself and his followers. He defeats that death. Later, the forces of evil will amass themselves, not in an episode of wind and waves, but in the structured death-wish of the best religion of the world, in the counter-terrorism violence of the best law of the world, and in the common consent of the general public. Jesus is destroyed. The Cross is the storm-centre of history. Christ's resurrection is the more complete exorcism, the cosmic muzzling of the powers of darkness. Now it is the risen Christ who is with us.

The disciples of Christ will find themselves in the storm. But many others of us will not be actually there, or at least we will not be there all the time. For much of the time, we will be spectators – all too frequent spectators, in these days of mass visual communication – of the terrors and traumas of our colleagues in discipleship. There they are, in the storms of Zimbabwe, Darfur, Afghanistan. And they will be there because of their calling to follow Christ. Otherwise, they could be peacefully sleeping in their beds. But remember Martin Luther King's version of the story of Rip van Winkel; when van Winkel went up into the hills to sleep for forty years, the flag over the land was that of George III; when he came down, the flag was that of George Wash-ington. "He had been sleeping through a revolution." So it may be with those who keep clear of the storm-centres of history.

In the days when Mark was writing, the followers of Jesus were well aware of the powers of the demonic. The systems of both Judaism and Rome were threatening to overwhelm the little boat of discipleship. In ch. 13 of his Gospel, Mark spells out the environment of disorder, of betrayal, of death, which the disciples of Jesus were experiencing within a few decades of his resurrection. They were experiencing the storms which he had experienced before them. Once again, the demons were claiming the mechanisms of power in their attempts to destroy the agents of the truth of God. The Gospel tells us, not that we shall never have to face these powers, but that we shall not be mastered by them.

The powers of evil still claim the mechanisms of power in our world, to subvert the programme of God's kingdom and to oppress the poorest of his children. The great structures of economic power con-tinue to ensure that wealth is absorbed from the labours of the poor to add to the riches of the privileged – exactly as in the colonial system by which Rome taxed the poor citizens of Jesus' nation. Does Jesus call for the destruction of Caesar? Does he put all the blame on the opera-tors of power? The principalities and powers that so corrupt the peace of the world are not the fault of a few malign individuals. Even the cruel system of apartheid was operated by "normal" human beings.

To me, Captain B of the South African Security Police was a real bastard. In repeated interrogations he gave me hell – and much worse to many others. But on one tense occasion, my wife noticed that he wore a wedding ring. I can't think of anything more weird than the picture of a woman finding delight in being in bed with Captain B. But he was a "normal" man doing a job within a demonic structure. He was a victim of the system, as much as those who were his victims. That was the insight underlying Desmond Tutu's commitment to the Truth and Reconciliation Commission. And if there is to be a place for me in the kingdom, I will not want it unless there is a place for Cap-tain B as well. In Christ's work of exorcism, we see again and again his skill in attacking the evil while cherishing the evil's victims and agents.

The language of demons makes it possible thus to oppose evil without becoming agents of evil ourselves.

The great powers that rule our contemporary world, the powers of finance, of land-possession, of enslavement of the poor, do give the impression of being mindless automatic mechanisms. So do the massive influences which drive nations into the madness of competing in nuclear weaponry, which stimulate the idolatry of consumerism, which measure a person's status by the size of their carbon footprint. These are very similar in their effect to the meteorological powers that experts can try to predict but are ineffective to control.

Many years ago, a stockbroker bewailed to me his despair at the madness of the market; it fell to me to suggest, very hesitatingly, that the movements of the market were actually caused not by mindless forces but by apparently intelligent persons trying to make responsible decisions. But certainly, the effect of the market upon most of us is that of a mindless, perverse, and capricious power that is out of human control and which victimises ordinary people who are outside the in-group of the controlling operators. This is very close to the biblical idea of "demon". It is also very close to the more modern experience of witchcraft. Both in the Gospel story, and in the experience of more recent missionaries, when the servants of God are consciously seeking God's kingdom in the world, the powers of darkness will converge; they will seek to claim the apparently mindless forces and powers in opposition. Our discipleship of Christ may well appear to make things worse. We may have the effect of stimulating the powers of evil to step up their efforts. So our discipleship will not immunise us; but Christ will be there with us. He will be alongside those in other boats who are caught up in the same storm. And that is a major part of the meaning of salvation.

Our forebears in Christian discipleship knew about these things. They prayed for deliverance from the powers of darkness. Modern Western Christianity has submitted to a spiritual censorship, based in academic propriety and religious gentility. Faced with the terrors of the 21st century, we need to claim our discipleship of a Master who can face up to the demonic structures that oppress us and say, "Be muzzled!" I make no apology for including in my daily prayer a verse from St Patrick's Breastplate which, in many details, can connect with the demands of our condition.

> Against all Satan's spells and wiles,
> Against false words of heresy,
> Against the knowledge that defiles,
> Against the heart's idolatry,

Against the wizard's evil craft,
Against the death-wound and the burning,
The choking wave, the poisoned shaft,
Protect me, Christ, till thy returning.[1]

Amen: come, Lord Jesus.

---

[1] For a practical exposition of St Patrick's Breastplate for our times, see John D. Davies, *A Song for Every Morning*, London: Canterbury Press, 2008.

4

Highly Unusual Ideological Magic

ANDREW PARKER

Mark's story is about a nature miracle. As such it presents us with a problem. Let's face it, you can't speak of the nature miracles as events that actually happened and be taken seriously these days unless you happen to be in some sort of religious meeting. For public discourse is only possible if everyone is on an equal footing. You can, at a pinch, have a public debate about whether the nature miracles could have happened but you cannot have such a debate *on the basis that they happened*. It is, of course, perfectly permissible for religious devotees to have private conversations in which the assumption is that Jesus' nature miracles took place as described. However, in public debate such an assumption is out of the question, and rightly so, for here the basis of conversation is what everyone shares, namely, common experience which does not include such things as nature miracles.

My problem is not simply that I have no desire to engage in private religious conversation but also that a lifetime's study of the Bible has convinced me that the majority of biblical writers demonstrate no such desire either. Their vision is characteristically public and ideological, not private and religious. They would have rejected out of hand any suggestion that they were involved in matters of concern only to those who had received religious revelation. They would have seen such a suggestion as a trivialisation of what they were on about which involved the responsibility of all human beings and not just of those who had been privileged with religious eyes to see. This being the case my first question is whether Mark presents his story as part of a private religious conversation or as part of a public ideological[1] debate. To put it bluntly does he put forward the miracle of the stilling of the storm as Jesus' exploitation of his special relationship with God – a matter which, if it were the case, we would be obliged to take on trust – or does he present it as a manifestation of power which resulted from Jesus' adoption of a particular ideological perspective and which would have been as plain as a pikestaff for all to see?

Mark's story involves a crossing of Lake Gennesaret and tells how Jesus fell asleep exhausted on the cushion in the stern when suddenly a storm blew up which threatened to sink the boat. The disciples, experienced fishermen, started to panic waking their passenger and scolding him for being oblivious of their plight. In their terror they looked to him to deal with the situation, ignoring the fact that it was they who had the requisite knowledge and experience. Jesus commanded the wind to cease and when the storm blew itself out asked them why they had all panicked showing such a sad lack of faith. The disciples for their part were dumbstruck wondering about this man whom even the winds and waves obeyed.

Let us for the moment forget what we have been told the Bible says and take it on trust both that Mark was aware the laws of nature couldn't be broken and that he wanted to communicate something that was evidently the case. Given such a perspective then clearly his story is about human charisma, its basic point being the incredible difference some people make in a tight situation. We are all aware of this phenomenon. Take for example the accounts of the battle of Waterloo which claim that the Duke of Wellington almost single-handedly kept the British lines from breaking by constantly moving around, exhibiting his presence and uttering brief words of encouragement. It would be a great mistake, of course, to leave it simply at that since there are clearly different forms of charisma, that manifested by the Duke of Wellington at the battle of Waterloo being rather different to that displayed by Jesus in Mark's story. My thesis is that charisma is a function of ideology: that the adoption of different world-views results in the production of different kinds of magnetism. On this basis let us examine Mark's story to see what kind of magnetism he attributes to Jesus.

In our experience, of course, most examples of human charisma involve a conservative ("blue") ideology. The leader inspires others by

---

[1] Since this word "ideology" causes much confusion these days let me make it quite clear that I use it narrowly to mean the way in which a person's world-view is *politically* coloured. This after all is the way in which the word is used in common parlance. We say, for example, that one individual has a conservative ideology and another a socialist ideology, thereby indicating that we see their ideas as politically coloured either "blue" or "red".

taking responsibility and, in return, demands unflinching obedience, loyalty and belief. Indeed this hierarchical model is so firmly fixed in our heads that we tend to take conservative magnetism as the only kind which exists. But is this true? It is often wrongly supposed that Jesus was the only person in the Gospels to perform miracles. In fact it is clear he expected those he healed to become healers in their turn, miracle-working not being a hierarchical exercise in his estimation. In Mark's story we can identify this anti-hierarchical attitude in Jesus' criticism of the disciples. If he had been working with a conservative ideology he would have expected them to turn to him as soon as difficulties arose and he would never have censured them for doing so. But this is not all. Had Jesus been a conservative leader one would have expected Mark's story to tell of a victory against the elements achieved through collective valour operating under inspired command. This is far from being what we actually get, which is simply a claim that Jesus demonstrated his mastery over the situation. As I see it Jesus' words "Be still!" tell of an attitude totally at variance with that displayed by Wellington at Waterloo. They portray Jesus certainly as acting somewhat *like* a conservative leader in that he shows no trace of fear. However, they give the impression that this was not due to Jesus' adoption of a hierarchical role in which a display of fearlessness is a necessary requisite that goes, as it were, with the job.

Rather they hint that his demeanour was due to the fact that he operated without any illusions embracing the truth that it is not a man's job in life to be in control of the situation but rather to make of the situation what he can while he is able to do so. It was this world-view, it seems to me, that created Jesus' particular charisma and which communicated itself to everyone around him. Mark's story tells how his sheer presence as one holding such a belief[2] enabled the disciples to pull themselves together and demonstrate what they were capable of and, before they knew it, the storm had been successfully weathered, as indeed it would have been without waking Jesus if they too had had the right attitude. Critics will say that such a reading reduces the impact of a story which tells of the disciples' astonishment that even the winds and the waves obeyed Jesus. However, it is important to understand that in the ancient Near East stories of nature miracles and tales of magic were the stock-in-trade of those who sought to describe people's ideological charisma and the effect they had on others and on the situation around them. Consequently such a story should be seen for what it is and not misunderstood as an analytical description of what took place one day out on the lake.

---

[2] Ideological belief, of course, not religious belief.

Given this basic understanding of Mark's story we now have to see if we can make anything more of it using Practice Interpretation; which is to say by reading it in the light of our own personal experience. Here is my offering.

In the early seventies I was sent to run a centre of the French Protestant Industrial Mission in a small town of Nemours situated fifty miles south of Paris. I had been told not to engage in any paternalist activity but to encourage people within the community to become active in solving their own problems. Quite soon a small team of local activists joined me, some of whom were Christian while others were Marxists[3] who found that the centre's new orientation fitted in with their own projects. There were four or five of us who lived permanently on site, however, at the weekends we were joined by quite a number of other young people. Some were students from Paris and others were young adults from the locality. Everyone became involved in different activities and discussion groups and in the evening after a meal prepared and enjoyed together bedded down where they could find a space. Since my own room was quite apart from the rest it was the other team members who saw to the night-time arrangements and, of course, discussions would sometimes go on far into the night.

On one occasion at about three o'clock in the morning one of the team members woke me to say that everything was in a terrible commotion. He begged me to come and help since there was nothing anyone could do. A young Maghrebian who had terrible personal problems and who had become a real social outcast has got himself drunk and had run amuck. All the young people staying in the centre, including the other team members, had tried to calm him down, to no avail. He had eventually run off and they had all gone after him since they were afraid he would get into trouble with the police. They had eventually managed to escort him back to the premises but since he was still acting up they had him pinned to the ground in the courtyard around which the centre itself was built. I went downstairs wondering how I should deal with the problem to find the young man with three people sitting on top of him and everyone else milling around in their nightwear. I sat down on a convenient bollard to take stock of the situation. What struck me was the noise. Everyone was telling me what had happened and arguing about what should be done. Surveying this scene something vague out of my own past suddenly hit me, making me realise what the basis of the problem was. I told everyone to go back to their beds and leave the youngster with me. At first they were reluctant to go since the young man had been behaving quite violently. However, I insisted and they all eventually left, giving the young man

---

[3] Mostly Maoists in fact.

a dire warning that if he assaulted me he would have them to deal with in the morning.

When they had all withdrawn, leaving me alone with the young man now lying prone in the middle of the courtyard, I began quietly to explain to him his dilemma as I saw it. I told him that in the past I too had been a bit of an outsider who desperately longed to be accepted by a group as someone special. I told him that, like him, I too had fallen into the trap of trying to engage everyone's attention by the simple expedient of making a fool of myself only to find that having turned on the performance I didn't know how to turn it off again. In the middle of my discourse he began to become agitated. Suddenly he got up and ran out into the night, just as he had done before. I went after him pleading with him to stop, telling him that I could not run after him all over the town in the middle of the night. Eventually he had mercy on me and came to a halt on a bridge and I sat with him on the parapet overlooking the canal. This time I started by telling him he had no need to make himself out to be someone special since we all liked him for what he was in himself and not for anything else. As he sat there silently staring down at the canal I wondered if I was getting through to him. As I began rather desperately to repeat myself he suddenly looked up and asked if he could now return to his bed. With barely disguised relief I replied "Yes, of course!" and he ran back to the centre leaving me to follow more slowly though no less thankfully.

There is, I know, nothing particularly amazing about my story, which could surely be paralleled by anyone who has had to deal professionally with young people. If I have bothered to recount it, therefore, it is not for what happened that night but rather for what happened the next morning when the other team members collared me. They were desperate to know how I had pulled off the trick, which they reckoned had been something of a miracle. They had, after all, spent half the night trying unsuccessfully to deal with the young man, who had clearly been off his head. Yet barely five minutes after they had left him alone with me, fearing greatly for my safety, he had crept quietly back into his bed without saying anything, as docile as a lamb. For me, of course, there was nothing miraculous about the incident, as I tried to explain to them. However, nothing I could say would convince them and so I was left with the dubious satisfaction of knowing that, in their eyes at least, I had been responsible for a spot of magic the previous night.

The point of my telling this story is to suggest that at a very low level of interest it demonstrates the kind of charisma Jesus operated with on an altogether more important scale. As I see it that night in the centre of the French Protestant Industrial Mission in Nemours I managed to deal with the problem I was faced with only because of something I had remembered from my own past. It was this which enabled me to empathise with that young man, understand his behaviour and help him see a way out of the situation he had created for himself. If it had been possible for me, in spite of all of my glaring inadequacies, to achieve such an empathy guided by my desire to be a disciple of Jesus, then imagine what sort of an understanding and empathy Jesus himself must have been capable of and what "miracles" – as his followers would have described them – he must, thereby, have been able to perform.

5

Which Boat Are You In?

CHRISTOPHER BURDON

Mark's story of the storm at sea draws a vivid picture within an easily imagined land- and seascape and with an almost palpable sound of wind and waves. It has easily identifiable characters engaged in concise and plain dialogue, full of emotion – fear, and awe, and possibly faith. The passage therefore lends itself well to an imaginative exercise for individuals or groups – working, for instance, in the Ignatian tradition of the reader's imagining herself within the scene, perhaps in dialogue with Jesus, and leading to some action or decision outside the world of the text.

When the passage occurred in the Revised Common Lectionary (Year B, proper 7), it was an obvious candidate for imaginative listening in the small parish group committed to regular study of the following Sunday's Gospel reading. This was a group of churchgoers, relatively middle-class and middle-aged, who might be expected to move fairly instinctively to a pious and positive response to the story. In most cases this is indeed what happened; but not in all.

The passage was first read aloud in dramatic form, without any reference to its context in either the Marcan narrative or the hearers' lives or any consideration of its historicity. After the calming of the storm and the question, "Who then is this...?" there was an appropriate silence until the hearers were asked in turn to say where they pictured themselves within the story and what was their response to the events and to the disciples' final question.

Several of them predictably saw themselves in the boat with Jesus, interpreted in a straightforwardly allegorical way. There were indeed storms around the "boat" of home, family or church, and they reckoned with the reality of fears within it. Yet their faith, reinforced by this story, informed them that they were "safe with Jesus". He was the master of the boat, with power exceeding that of the world's waves, and these hearers' answer to the final question was unambiguous: "This is the Son of God, the Lord of earth and sea, our protector in the world."

Two other listeners likewise pictured themselves in the boat with Jesus, but their response to the events was very different. Jesus was not a reliable protector, nor was the God he represented. He was, literally, not vigilant, for when there was desperate need he lay in the oblivion of sleep. Jesus has to be woken and brings salvation only when pestered by the fearful crew, whom he then rebukes in a rather obscure way. So whilst there may be power in his presence and his words, the final question remains unanswered. It is not a power that can be depended on, and the "boat" in which we face the world's storms remains a precarious one.

One more listener found himself unable to get as far as the final question, let alone to answer it. "I wasn't in that boat with Jesus and the disciples. I was one of the crowd who got into one of those other boats. I don't know what's happened to us."

If the exercise of imagination is allowed, then – if the author's intention cannot be ascertained or cannot be allowed to determine the text's meaning – we are left with a multiplicity of meanings and varying degrees of assurance and faith. These echo perhaps the differing interpretations and degrees of faith in the boat or boats within the story. For this story is about the Messiah and the community around him, but, even when moored more firmly in its canonical context, it does not explicitly proclaim an accessible saviour or a united church.

So, building on those responses, I am tackling this passage as a practical exercise in what could rather pompously be called "pluralist ecclesiology". To talk of any kind of ecclesiology in relation to a gospel where notions of community are so ambiguous and where the word *ekklēsia* does not occur might seem fanciful. Nevertheless, I shall defend though also qualify the typology of Mark's boat as what soon became seen as "the ark of the church"; that is, the place where the disciples are "with Jesus" and might therefore be expected to be safe and even apart from "the world" – as, in a rather ambiguous way, they are in this story.

The typology is not very satisfactory (from an orthodox ecclesiastical point of view) because of at least three conundrums in the passage, picked up by some of those group members. I shall address these in turn. First, unlike the ideal Church, Mark's boat is emphatically *not* a place of communion, peace and understanding. Secondly, Jesus emerges as saviour only when the sailors are *in extremis:* up to then he is asleep. And thirdly, if the boat with Jesus in it is the Church, what about the "other boats" mentioned in 4.36b?

1. Ark of Salvation or Boat of Confusion?

Whatever its historical and redactional origins, those group members were right that, in its present form and in Mark as much as in Matthew, this is a story crying out for an allegorical reading. Though it is a miracle story and an exorcism story, a Christological and perhaps an epiphany story, it is more than these. It is a "church story" too. Details like the cry "we are perishing" (*apollumetha*), the move from the "great gale" (*lailaps megalē*) to the "great calm" (*galēnē megalē*), the symbolism of the boat itself, all point to a companionship between the disciples and the one who is revealed once more in the way that John first introduced him, "the stronger one" – in this case, one stronger than that other sleeping sailor Jonah. And in varying degrees, the readers share that watery companionship. Austin Farrer observed that this ecclesial and baptismal symbolism is not some allegory drawn out of a doctrine and turned into narrative, but rather facts that "fall into such a pattern that, like true works of God, they become expressive".[1] Again, Ernest Best sees a natural trajectory from Mark's sea stories where Jesus is deliverer to "the development within the later church of the ship as a symbol for the Christian community", adding, "indeed, this may already underlie Mark's use, for the image may be pre-Christian and Jewish and have been taken over".[2]

But the allegory need not bring with it a complacent or triumphalist ecclesiology. That has certainly played its part in the Church's self-understanding – an ark like Noah's sailing calmly over the waters of the world, its chosen inhabitants the only ones to be saved. But the first explicit instance of the Christian "ark" typology is based on this gospel story and is far from triumphalist, or at least envisages triumph only at the eschaton. In the middle of an arcane argument as to whether the apostles were baptised, Tertullian remarks that "that little

---

[1] A.M. Farrer, *A Study in St Mark*, Westminster: Dacre Press, 1951, pp. 87–88.

[2] E. Best, *Following Jesus: Discipleship in the Gospel of Mark*, Sheffield: JSOT Press, 1981, p. 232; cf. D. Nineham, *Saint Mark*, Pelican Gospel Commentaries; Harmondsworth: Penguin, p. 147; C.E.B. Cranfield, *The Gospel according to St Mark*, Cambridge Greek Testament Commentary; Cambridge: Cambridge University Press, p. 175. Morna Hooker is much more wary of allegory, seeing the "main point" of the story as Christological – "that which is implied by the final question of the disciples, 'Who then is this?'" M.D. Hooker, *Gospel according to St Mark*, Black's NT Commentaries; London: A. & C. Black, 1991, p. 138. For a summary, see J. Gnilka, *Evangelium nach Markus*, EKK; Zürich: Benziger, 1978, I.197-198.

ship [*navicula*] presented a type of the Church, because on the sea, which means this present world [*saeculo*], it is being tossed about by the waves, which means persecutions and temptations, while our Lord in his long-suffering is as it were asleep, until at the last times he is awakened by the prayers of the saints to calm the world and restore tranquillity to his own".[3] The church is not temple or palace, founded on dry land, but *navicula*, that is, something in transition. "Let us go across to the other side", says Jesus at the beginning of the story; and the place where you are with Jesus is mobile, one where you can expect danger and swamping.

So it is entirely appropriate that, although the storm is quelled by Jesus, the story ends with an expression of real terror. There may be an impressive "great calm" but it doesn't calm the disciples: it moves them perhaps to a Christological question but hardly to a Christological confession. The phrase "feared a great fear" (*ephobēthēsan phobon megan*) of 4.41 is akin to the women's final *ephobounto* in 16.8: both are failures of perception and only potentially occasions of awe. In the next main boat story, where Jesus is not in the boat but was going to pass by them in the storm (6.47–52), the climax is far from confessional; instead, "they were utterly astounded", with total lack of understanding and "hardened heart". The final boat story, with its confused dialogue about bread (8.14–21), demonstrates an even deeper failure of understanding on the part of the disciples – hearts hardened, eyes unseeing, ears unhearing – and harsh frustration on the part of Jesus.

If then this *navicula* is the Church, it's not a very impressive one. It is not a place of communion but of flamboyant non-communion. When, later in the story, the disciples' perhaps rhetorical question is put directly by Jesus himself and is answered by one of them, the presumably correct answer is immediately concealed (8.29–30). Later still, the actual proclamation of the "answer" is in the mouth of a foreign soldier, though even this could actually be in the form of a question, or even a sarcastic comment (15.39). The Church's Christology here is seen as built on waves, not on firm ground. And the "safe with Jesus" interpretation of the story, while superficially appropriate as well as attractive, is actually seen on closer reading to resist the grain of the text. For these disciples are barely safe and fulfil their calling to be "with Jesus" (3.14) only in the most literal physical sense.

2. The Sleeping Saviour

Two of the hearers in our group had indeed sensed this uncertainty. For the second conundrum that undermines the boat as an imperme-

[3] Tertullian, *De Baptismo Liber* 12, ed. E. Evans; London: SPCK, 1964, pp. 28-29.

able ark of salvation is the sleep of Jesus. Although he is the one who takes the initiative for the journey to "the other side", when it actually begins he is physically and grammatically the object (*paralambanousin auton*, 4.36), and when the storm arises he is oblivious to the sailors' plight. Tertullian's allegorical and eschatological reading of the sleep of Jesus, which does not prevent the Church's being tossed by the waves of persecution and temptation, is germane here and is perhaps familiar to the experience of many Christians whether in his time or Mark's or our own. For the community of believers is not one permanently sitting at the feet of its teacher or gathered round his table: as in this Gospel, the teacher is often absent or ahead, and when present often riddling. We are dealing with a little fishing boat, not a Cunard liner; nor with a place of certainty, clearly enclosed from the world or sea, but with one of frailty, invaded by the waves. It is a community of *faith* rather than of knowledge. Jesus' question at 4.40 implies that faith is the antithesis of fear. And perhaps, as many interpreters have suggested, the real sign of faith in this story is not the response to the miracle or the question of the disciples but the sleep of Jesus himself – a secure resting on the cushion even when drowning seems imminent.[4] The sleep may also be an image of the sleeping divine sovereign himself.[5]

Elsewhere in Mark's Gospel, and especially in chapter 13, faith requires alert seeing and hearing, the vigilance of those who do not know when their enemy may strike. But here faith is expressed in rest, in *shabbat*. As later in Jerusalem, the faithful one does not act but is acted upon, which is perhaps another way of saying that faith is not a "work". Faith is the sleep, if not of reason, then of fear. The more sceptical members of the group who questioned the reliability of the sleeping saviour were, in this sense, faithful as well as alert readers. For Jesus is not obviously in control nor even hearing his companions' cry, and his question – or Mark's (4.40) – carries with it the implication that the way of faith does not lie in dependence on nor in confession of nor in homage to a saviour: it lies rather in fearlessly grasping hold of the story oneself and going ahead in the saviour's absence, in the trustfulness of sleep.

---

[4] Cf. Ps 4:8. So Gnilka, *Evangelium nach Markus*, I.195; F.J. Moloney, *Gospel of Mark: A Commentary*, Peabody, Mass.: Hendrickson, 2002, p. 99.

[5] So J. Marcus, *Mark 1–8*, Anchor Bible; New York: Doubleday, 2000, p. 338. Cf. the calls to God to "awake" at Pss 35.23; 44.23; 59.5; Isa 51.9-10; and his waking to action at Ps 78.65.

3. The Other Boats

This leads to the third conundrum of the passage, concerning the boundaries of the boat or church or community of disciples. It is the odd aside – omitted by both Matthew and Luke – "and other boats were with him" (*kai alla ploia ēn met' autou,* 4.36). This is where one solitary hearer in our group found himself, adrift in some confusion and fear. We are not told who were in these "other boats" or what happened to them. Were they destroyed in the storm? Did they share in the deliverance wrought by Jesus' exorcism of it? Did Mark retain this obscure and perhaps historical detail to point to witnesses of the miracle, or add it "to heighten the drama of the impending disaster" or to allow his readers "to imagine themselves within the story", as some interpreters tentatively surmise?[6] A trawl through other commentaries shows most interpreters dismissing the significance of the phrase. It is an inconsequential if "probably a genuine reminiscence", or a comment with "no relevance to the story as it now stands", or simply obscure, or even a textual mistake because of an omitted *ouk*.[7] Of these interpretations, only those of Marcus and possibly van Iersel reckon with the possibility of the reader's sailing in one of these boats, or the possibility that they are the actual location of Mark's implied reader; and certainly none, any more than Mark himself, suggests where that would take him or her.

Now Mark may be enigmatic but I find it hard to see him as careless. The confused sailors (or readers) in the rest of the flotilla deserve to be taken seriously. It may be that they are part of a larger if less identifiable group of followers of Jesus than those "with him" in the principal boat – which has serious implications in turn for those eager to define the boundaries of the Church. Thus Simon Légasse, positing that Mark 4.36b is a "vestige of Mark's source", is nevertheless unwilling to "believe that the evangelist would not have drawn some benefit from this", and speculates:

> … one might align it with an analogous scenario depicted later (6.32–33): instead of following Jesus on foot to get round the lake,

---

[6] So, respectively, E. Schweizer, *Good News according to Mark,* trans. D.H. Madvig. London: SPCK, 1971, p. 107; B.M.F. van Iersel, *Mark: A Reader-Response Commentary,* trans. W.H. Bisscheroux, London: T. & T. Clark, 1998, p. 194; Marcus, *Mark 1–8,* p. 333.

[7] So, respectively, V. Taylor, *Gospel according to St Mark,* 2nd edn, London: Macmillan, 1966, p. 274; R.A. Guelich, *Mark 1–8:26,* Word Biblical Commentary; Dallas: Word Books, 1989, pp. 265-66; Hooker, *Mark,* p. 139; E. Lohmeyer, *Das Evangelium des Markus,* Göttingen: Vandenhoeck & Ruprecht, 1957, p. 90. Cf. W.L. Lane, *Gospel according to St Mark,* Grand Rapids: Eerdmans, 1974, pp. 174-75; B. Witherington, *Gospel of Mark: A Socio-Rhetorical Commentary,* Grand Rapids: Eerdmans, 2001, p. 174. For a summary, see R. Pesch, *Das Markusevangelium,* Freiburg: Herder, 1976, I.270.

these people use vessels. Both instances give Mark a way of empha-
sising the immense success of this Jesus, from whom the crowds
cannot bear to be separated.[8]

The "crowd" – whether in the other boats or on the hillside – is not
in this interpretation an uninvolved mass or mere narrative foil to the
main action. Francis Moloney more boldly picks up the phrase "with
him" (*met' autou*) applied to the other boats. He sees it as aligning –
though not identifying – the sailors in these boats with the twelve who
were called by Jesus to be *met' autou* (3.14) and with the demoniac
who asked to remain *met' autou* (5.18). They are likely to be (narra-
tively, if not historically) those referred to earlier in the same chapter as
"those who were about him with the twelve" (4.10). So Moloney
concludes:

> The additional boats indicate that Jesus's entourage is increasing. Al-
> though the narrative which follows only focuses upon those in the
> boat with Jesus, the judgement of Jesus and the ongoing failure of
> the disciples, described at the end of the pericope, embrace this lar-
> ger gathering of people.[9]

These are disciples who are "with" Jesus yet not with him, for they
are in separate boats. Which suggests – if we are to retain an allegorical
and ecclesiological reading of this story – that the entourage of Jesus,
the Church if you will, is in many ways indistinct, that it is not enclosed or numbered or indeed united. Access to the community is easy,
but remaining firmly in it is hard – perhaps all the harder because of
the indistinctness of the boundaries and its foundation not on rock but
on water (here, Mark is radically different from Matthew, and indeed
from John and Paul). Moloney continues:

> Despite their being the privileged 'insiders' of 4.1–34, [the disciples]
> remain 'outside' the mystery of Jesus. Nevertheless, the failing disci-
> ples, those in the boat with Jesus and also those in the other boats, as
> Jesus's entourage increases (v. 36), have been invited to 'cross over'
> the terrors of the sea which he conquers. They witness Jesus per-
> form his mighty works for the first time in a Gentile land. As hith-
> erto, the disciples will continue to be 'with him' across the sea, in
> Gerasa (5.1–20).[10]

[8] S. Légasse, *L'Evangile de Marc*, Lectio Divina 5; Paris : Cerf, 1997, I.309-310 (my
translation). But contrast Best's judgement that 4:36a "serves to emphasis the separation
of Jesus and the disciples from the crowd. It is a miracle for the community of the
disciples and not for the unevangelised crowd" (*Following Jesus*, p. 231).
[9] Moloney, *Gospel of Mark*, p. 98.
[10] Moloney, *Gospel of Mark*, p. 101.

The fluid community is formed, reformed and transformed on its fluid foundation in the company, close or less close, of Jesus the sailor. Whether this brings any comfort to the fragmented and storm-tossed fleet of the Anglican Communion I am not sure. But something of this conundrum of faith and this baptismal challenge is expressed by that astute religious poet Leonard Cohen:

> ... And Jesus was a sailor
> When he walked upon the water
> And he spent a long time watching
> From his lonely wooden tower.
> And when he knew for certain
> Only drowning men could see him
> He said, "All men will be sailors then
> Until the sea shall free them."
> But he himself was broken
> Long before the sky would open,
> Forsaken, almost human,
> He sank beneath your wisdom like a stone.
> And you want to travel with him
> And you want to travel blind
> And you think maybe you'll trust him
> For he's touched your perfect body with his mind.[11]

[11] Leonard Cohen, "Suzanne" (1966).

6

Women in the Boat?

SUSAN MILLER

Introduction

In Mark 4 Jesus and his disciples leave the crowd, and cross the Sea of Galilee at night. During their boat journey a great storm arises, and waves beat into the boat so that it fills with water. The disciples wake Jesus, and he stills the storm. The disciples cross the Sea of Galilee in order to take their mission to new areas, and the boat journey acts as a metaphor for discipleship. The strong wind and the waves represent opposition to the mission, and the stilling of the storm indicates the power of Jesus to bring help to his disciples. The account acts as an encouragement to the Markan community. Mark, however, does not make any specific references to women in the narrative. In Mark, there is no description of the call of a woman disciple, and women are not included in the group of twelve disciples chosen to be with Jesus (3.13–19). The twelve male disciples are portrayed as Jesus' constant companions. What significance has the account of the stilling of the storm for women?

Throughout Mark's Gospel women are present in the crowds that listen to Jesus' teaching. Women are praised when Jesus describes those who sit around him listening to his teaching as his brother, sister and mother (3.31–35). The woman with the flow of blood, moreover, emerges from a crowd to seek healing, and Jesus praises this woman for her faith (5.34). In Mark 4 Jesus teaches such a large crowd that he enters a boat while the people remain on the shore. Jesus teaches the crowd the parable of the sower, and afterwards the Twelve and some others approach Jesus for the interpretation of this parable. These people receive additional teaching: "To you has been given the secret of the kingdom of God, but for those outside, everything comes in parables" (4.11). At the end of Jesus' teaching on parables the narrator draws a distinction between the crowd who are taught in parables and his disciples who receive explanations. In this passage the term 'disciples' refers to a wider group than the Twelve, and may include women (4.34).

Mark's narrative focuses on the twelve male disciples, and there is no specific mention of the presence of women in the boat with Jesus. Mark, however, describes the presence of "other boats" (4.36), and these boats are puzzling because they play no part in the narrative. Why does Mark include a reference to these boats? It is possible that Mark wishes to imply that other disciples take part in this journey. The boats are described as being "with him," and this phrase recalls the commission of the twelve disciples who are chosen to be "with Jesus" (3.14). In this way women are likely to be present in the other boats who set out across the Sea of Galilee. In the account of the stilling of the storm Mark is concerned with the experiences of Jesus and the disciples within one boat but the boat journey may thus have a representative function for all disciples.

1. The Boat Journeys

At the beginning of the account Jesus is sleeping at the stern during the storm. The disciples ask Jesus, "Do you not care that we are perishing?" (4.38). The disciples are afraid that they will die, and that Jesus will not intervene to help them. Jesus rebukes the wind, and he commands the sea to be silent, and this description is reminiscent of the exorcism accounts. Jesus "rebukes" demons (1.25; 3.12; 9.24), and he also silences an unclean spirit during the exorcism in the synagogue at Capernaum (1.25). In the account of the stilling of the storm the language associated with exorcisms implies a demoniac opposition to Jesus. In the Old Testament the sea is associated with the forces of chaos and evil. Jesus, however, has the power to overcome this opposition, and he stills the storm so that there is a great calm.

The miraculous power of Jesus is similar to the power of God over the elements in the Old Testament (Pss 46.3; 89.9; 107.29 and Isa 51.9–10), and God rebukes the sea in Pss 18.15; 104.7; 106.9; Isa 50.2 and Nah 1.4. The account of the stilling of the storm depicts a high Christology, and Jesus is attributed with the authority of God over nature. Mark focuses on the responses of the disciples to Jesus' miraculous action. Jesus asks the disciples, "Why are you afraid? Have you still no faith?" His question suggests that he expects the disciples to have faith. The account raises the issue of the nature of faith. Are the disciples expected to have faith that Jesus will save them from the storm? Jesus, however, criticises the actions of the disciples in waking him, and his response suggests that the disciples are expected to remain faithful in the midst of the storm.

After Jesus stills the storm, the disciples are greatly afraid, and their fear is an indication of their awe at the miracle they have witnessed. On the other hand their fear also has negative associations. As Morna Hooker points out, fear is often depicted as the opposite of faith (5.36; 6.50; 10.32; 16.8).[1]

The disciples question one another about Jesus' identity, "Who then is this, that even the wind and sea obey him?" (4.41). The miracle thus creates a division between Jesus and his disciples, and the disciples speak to one another rather than directly to Jesus. Mark ends this narrative without a resolution to the disciples' debate, and Mark's audience is left with the question of Jesus' identity.

The account of the stilling of the storm is one of two boat journeys in which a strong opposing wind arises. The second boat journey also takes place in the evening, and the disciples find it difficult to make any progress. During the fourth watch Jesus approaches his disciples walking on the water, and he wishes to go past them. Jesus' action is disturbing. Why does he not come to the aid of his disciples? The disciples are terrified, and believe he is a ghost but Jesus replies, "Take heart, it is I; do not be afraid" (6.50). This passage also points to Jesus' identity, since the phrase "It is I" occurs in the account of the revelation of God to Moses in Exodus 3.14. In this narrative Jesus enters the boat and the wind subsides. As in the first boat journey, Jesus is concerned about the fear of the disciples.

Each boat journey describes a mission to the "other side," and is related to the mission of the discipleship community. On the first boat journey the disciples are travelling to the gentile area of the Decapolis, and on the second boat journey Jesus sends the disciples on ahead of him to Bethsaida, a mainly gentile city. In Mark 13 Jesus teaches his disciples that they are to carry out a mission to all nations (13.10). Ched Myers notes the storm occurs in the midst of the journeys, and he proposes that the Markan community experiences difficulties in integrating Jewish and gentile members.[2] The journeys represent the progression of Jesus' mission to other lands, and the narratives suggest that the opposition the disciples experience is particularly associated with the gentile mission. These accounts contain high Christology, and

---

[1] M.D. Hooker, *The Gospel according to St Mark*, London: A. & C. Black, 1991, p. 140.

[2] C. Myers, *Binding the Strong Man. A Political Reading of Mark's Story of Jesus*, Maryknoll: Orbis, 1997, p. 197.

it is possible that the disciples' belief in Christ may be the reason why they face persecution.[3] The boat journeys associate the mission of the disciples with a struggle between faith and fear. On the level of the Markan community the disciples are afraid that they will experience persecution during their mission, and these passages stress the power of Jesus to overcome opposition.

2. Women Disciples

The account of the stilling of the storm gives the impression that Jesus travels with a group of twelve male disciples who are chosen to be with him (3.14), and there are no references to women disciples in the opening chapters and the central section of the Gospel. Mark, however, mentions of a group of women disciples for the first time at the crucifixion of Jesus (15.40–41). These women have followed and served Jesus in Galilee before accompanying him to Jerusalem. In the Passion Narrative Judas betrays Jesus, and the other members of the Twelve flee at the arrest of Jesus (14.50). Peter, the leading disciple, denies Jesus three times. The male disciples are afraid that they will be arrested and put to death, and they are not present at the crucifixion.

Mark names three women: Mary Magdalene, Mary the mother of James and Joses, and Salome. Kathleen Corley suggests that only the three named women constantly accompany Jesus.[4] Mark describes two groups of women: one group of women has followed and served Jesus in Galilee, and the second group has joined his company in order to travel to with him to Jerusalem. The names of the three women are recorded because they are the key witnesses to the death and burial of Jesus, and they are the disciples who will go to the empty tomb and hear the news of Jesus' resurrection.

Why has Mark mentioned these women at such a late stage in the Gospel? Has Mark intended to conceal their presence? Winsome Munro argues that Mark only refers to the women because the male disciples have now fled.[5] Mark, however, describes the women in terms of discipleship, since the women have followed Jesus in Galilee, the starting-place of Jesus' mission. The verb "to follow" is associated with the call of the male disciples. Peter and Andrew follow Jesus (1.18), and the tax collector, Levi, is also described as following Jesus (2.14). Mark includes a call to the disciples and the crowd to follow him on the way

---

[3] J. Marcus, *Mark 1–8. A New Translation with Introduction and Commentary*, AB 27; New York: Doubleday, 2000, pp. 338-39.

[4] K.E. Corley, "Slaves, Servants and Prostitutes: Gender and Social Class in Mark", in A-J. Levine, ed., *A Feminist Companion to Mark*, Sheffield: Sheffield Academic Press, 2001, p. 198.

[5] W. Munro, "Women Disciples in Mark?" *CBQ* 44 (1982), pp. 225-41.

of the cross (8.31–34). The women have not only followed Jesus from Galilee to Jerusalem. They have continuously followed him in Galilee before going up to Jerusalem.

The women are also described as "serving" Jesus, and the basic meaning of the Greek verb *diakoneō* is to "to wait at table".[6] In an earlier account Simon's mother-in-law serves a meal to Jesus after she has been healed (1.31). Do the women disciples also prepare and serve meals during Jesus' mission? The women disciples, however, have accompanied Jesus on an itinerant mission. The group of disciples live at subsistence level, and rely on the hospitality of others. The women disciples would not have been able to cook and serve meals in traditional household roles. The women, moreover, are described as following "him" and serving "him". The use of the masculine singular pronoun "him" implies that the women serve Jesus alone rather than Jesus and the male disciples. In this way their service suggests a relationship of committed discipleship to Jesus.

On the way to Jerusalem Jesus teaches his disciples about the significance of service and the way of the cross. In this section the failures of the male disciples are emphasised. Peter recognises Jesus as the Messiah, and Jesus gives his first passion prediction. Peter does not accept the necessity of Jesus' suffering and death, and he attempts to dissuade Jesus from his mission. In response, Jesus calls Peter "Satan" because Peter is aligned with Satan who is known as the "opponent". Jesus' second passion prediction is followed by a debate among the disciples as to which one of them is the greatest (9.34), and Jesus then teaches his disciples that they should take the role of a servant, "Whoever wants to be first must be last of all and servant of all" (9.35). After the third passion prediction James and John seek the places of honour on either side of Jesus (10.35–45), and Jesus teaches them, "Whoever wishes to be first among you must be slave of all" (10.44).

Jesus defines his own mission in terms of service, "For the Son of Man came not to be served but to serve and to give his life a ransom for many" (10.45). Women are described as serving Jesus (1.31; 15.40–41) but the Twelve are never described as serving Jesus. As Mary Cotes notes, women and men both follow Jesus, but only the women understand that following Jesus involves service.[7] The women are particularly aligned with the service of Jesus in giving his life for others. The

---

[6] H. Beyer, *TDNT*, II, pp. 81-93.
[7] M. Cotes, "Following Jesus with the Women in Mark", in *Mark: Gospel of Action: Personal and Community Responses*, ed. J. Vincent, London: SPCK, 2006, p. 84.

hidden service of the women reflects the teaching of Jesus that disciples should place themselves last of all and servants of all.[8]

Mark 15.40–41 mentions the presence of women disciples in Galilee and their journey to Jerusalem. The description of the women implies that they have been members of the group of disciples throughout Jesus' mission. Although Mark does not refer to the women in the account of the stilling of the storm, it is possible that they are travelling in one of the other boats. In this case they would also experience the storm, and its miraculous ending. Mark's literary technique of specifically mentioning the women at the crucifixion, however, implies that the women are to be contrasted with the male disciples. The women remain faithful to Jesus after the male disciples have fled. They are the only witnesses of Jesus' death and burial, and they are the ones who go to the tomb.

3. The Visit of the Women to the Tomb

After the Sabbath has passed, Mary Magdalene, Mary, and Salome set out to anoint Jesus' body. At the tomb the women meet a young man who tells them that Jesus has been raised. The young man has the role of a divine messenger, who is waiting to give the women the news of the resurrection. The women are instructed to go and tell the disciples and Peter that Jesus is going ahead of them to Galilee, and they will see him there just as he told them (16.7). The women have been portrayed favourably in the Passion Narrative but this account challenges the earlier presentation because the women now flee from the tomb terrified to say anything to anyone.

Why does Mark end the Gospel in this way? The portrayal of the women recalls the portrayal of the male disciples in the boat journeys. Initially the women are amazed, and they leave the tomb "fearful and trembling" (16.8). Frequently, human beings are amazed at the miracles of Jesus (1.27; 2.12; 6.2; 7.37), and the same term of amazement describes the witnesses to the raising of Jairus's daughter (5.42). David Catchpole associates the phrase "fear and trembling" with the manifestation of God's power (cf. Job 4.12–16; Gen 4.12–16; 28.17; Ps 2.11).[9] The women are afraid in the same way that the disciples are greatly afraid after Jesus miraculously stills the storm. Now the women are afraid at the news of the resurrection. In both episodes fear points

---

[8] S. Miller, *Women in Mark's Gospel*, JSNTS 259; London: Continuum, 2004, p. 164.

[9] D. Catchpole, "The Fearful Silence of the Women at the Tomb: A Study in Markan Theology", *JTSA* 18 (1977), pp. 3-10.

to the transcendence of God, and the gulf between God and humanity is emphasised.

Nevertheless, the women's fear also has negative connotations because Mark 16.8 indicates that the women's fear prevents them from passing on the news of the resurrection. As we have seen, the disciples' fear is portrayed negatively on the boat journeys. Jesus criticises the disciples' fear and asks them if they still have no faith (4.41), and he tells them not to be afraid (6.50). Mark's portrayal of the women is related to his theory of the Messianic Secret. Throughout the Gospel human beings are instructed to keep silent about Jesus' miracles and his identity (1.25, 34, 44; 3.12; 5.43; 7.36; 8.26). At the transfiguration Jesus instructs his disciples to tell no one about what they have witnessed until the Son of Man has risen from the dead (9.9). The resurrection is thus presented as a turning point, and the women are now told to pass on the news of the resurrection to the disciples and to Peter.

The women are instructed to reconstitute the group of disciples, and to resume Jesus' mission. Mark associates the women with fear of persecution linked to their mission. In Mark 13 Jesus prophesies that his disciples will be brought to trial before councils, and governors and kings (13.9). During this period the disciples are to carry out a mission to all nations (13.10). They are not to worry beforehand about what they will say because the Holy Spirit will be given to them (13.11). Jesus teaches his disciples that discipleship involves the way of the cross, and the disciples will only see Jesus if they follow him (Mark 8.34). Discipleship involves facing suffering and death, but those who are willing to lose their lives will save their lives (8.35).

The male disciples fled at the arrest of Jesus (14.50) and now the women flee from the tomb (16.8). Elizabeth Struthers Malbon argues that both women and men are "fallible followers" who are unable to remain faithful to Jesus.[10] The women, however, have shown courage in their presence at the crucifixion of Jesus, and they are the key witnesses to the death and resurrection of Jesus. The future mission thus depends on the testimony of the women disciples. Why do the women and men find discipleship difficult? Mark emphasises that the fear of the disciples is related to the increasing persecution of the end of the age. The struggle between faith and fear reflects the eschatological conflict of the end-time.[11] The cosmic conflict of the end of the age is illu-

[10] E.S. Malbon, "Fallible Followers: Women and Men in the Gospel of Mark", *Semeia* 28 (1983), pp. 29-48.

[11] S. Miller, "'They Said Nothing to Anyone': The Fear and Silence of the Women at the Empty Tomb (Mk 16:1-8)", *Feminist Theology* 13 (2004), pp. 77-90.

strated in the narratives depicting storms that arise on the boat journeys. In the Passion Narrative Jesus prophesies that when the shepherd is struck the sheep will be scattered (14.27). Without the presence of Jesus, the disciples are unable to stay faithful. In the next verse he states that he will go before his disciples to Galilee after he has been raised (14.28). Jesus is portrayed as the shepherd who leads his disciples on their mission. The young man at the tomb repeats Jesus' prophecy that he is going before the disciples to Galilee, and that they will see him there. In this way Jesus will again become present to his disciples.

Conclusion

The boat journeys illustrate the ways in which Jesus is able to help his female and male disciples. Both journeys are concerned with the disciples' struggle between faith and fear (4.40–41; 6.50). On the first boat journey the absence of Jesus is suggested by the statement that he is sleeping in the stern of the boat, and Jesus wakes and stills the storm. On the second boat journey the disciples are sent on ahead while Jesus remains on the shore to pray. In both accounts Jesus is portrayed with the power of God over the natural elements, and he is able to intervene and calm the strong opposing winds. In Mark 16 the death of Jesus separates him from his disciples but the disciples may see the risen Jesus if they follow him to Galilee. The one who has power over the elements has suffered death but has been raised.

Our analysis of Mark 16 indicates that the women disciples feel the same sense of amazement and fear as the male disciples. The women have accompanied Jesus and the disciples, and they are part of the wider group of disciples who accompany Jesus on his boat journey. The boat journeys are depicted as metaphors of the mission of the disciples. Just as storms arise on the boat journeys, the disciples will experience persecution. According to this interpretation the women are "in the same boat" as the disciples. Jesus' miracles indicate that Jesus has the power to still the storm, and he has the power to overcome opposition to the disciples' mission. The presence of Jesus quells the storms on the boat journeys, and he will be present for the disciples who follow him on the way of the cross.

7

Rescuing "Unbelieving Believers"

NEIL RICHARDSON

In his study of faith in Mark's Gospel Christopher Marshall claims that Mark, in his version of the stilling of the storm, depicts the disciples as "unbelieving believers".[1] This judgement, I believe, is correct. Whereas in Matthew Jesus calls the disciples "people of little faith (*oligopistoi*)" (Matt 8.26), and in Luke he asks them "Where is your faith?" (Luke 8.25), in Mark he says to them, "Have you still no faith?" (v. 40)[2]. The implication is clear: in Matthew the disciples have only a little faith, in Luke they have (temporarily?) lost their faith, but in Mark they have none at all. This is a startling detail, particularly in view of the story's outcome – hence the title of this paper.

In his commentary on Mark, Edwin Broadhead suggests that in this story "the real crisis is found in the hearts of the disciples"[3]. His words acquire greater significance in the light of Mark's overall portrayal of the disciples. They appear to start off well enough. Jesus calls Peter, Andrew, James and John to follow him (1.14–18), and they do so. But the clearest, most positive affirmation of the privileged status of the twelve comes a little later in Mark's narrative:

> He went up the mountain and called to him those whom he wanted, and they came to him. And he appointed twelve, whom he also named apostles, to be with him ... (3.13–14).

---

[1] Christopher D. Marshall, *Faith as a Theme in Mark's Narrative*, Cambridge: Cambridge University Press, 1989 (quotation from p. 219 of the 1994 paperback edition). With this compare Marshall's conclusion, at the end of his discussion of the disciples' unbelief, that Mark is not implying a total absence of faith in the disciples (p. 218).

[2] The reading of *oupo* is to be preferred.

[3] Edwin K. Broadhead, *Mark*, Sheffield: Sheffield Academic Press, 2001, p. 50.

Yet there are early hints that they are not entirely with Jesus. At 1.36 Mark chooses a rather hostile-sounding verb (*katedioxen*), to describe how "Simon and those with him follow" (harass?) Jesus into his lonely place of prayer.[4] True, they are to be the privileged recipients of the mystery of the Kingdom (4.11; cf. 4.34), yet Jesus' question to them in this chapter sounds reproachful:

> "Do you not understand this parable? Then how will you understand all the parables?" (v. 13).

In subsequent sections of the Gospel, the picture gets worse. After the second feeding miracle, Jesus asks them if their hearts are "hardened" (8.17), using the very phrase used by the evangelist to describe the hostile observers of an earlier miracle in a synagogue (3.5). In the second half of the Gospel, the nearer Jesus comes to his cross, the worse his disciples become. It is hard to find a favourable reference to them, and their failures culminate in the apostasy and denial narrated in the Passion Story (14.50, 66–72).[5] So Marshall perhaps understates the disciples' rejection of the cross in his otherwise correct conclusion to his discussion of unbelief among the disciples:

> Mark does not portray discipleship as a steady progress from unbelief, through doubt to the inviolate certainty of faith, but as a constant to-and-froing between the values outlook of the *genea apistos*[6] and the values and perspective of God's rule.[7]

So the disciples followed Jesus without really believing in him, and, in this story, even though they were with Jesus, they still believed that the storm would kill them. In other words, there was a deep inconsistency in their discipleship. Their unbelief finds expression in their cry for help. It does not sound like the request of men who knew where salvation from the storm was to be found:

> "Teacher, do you not care that we are perishing?" (v. 38c).[8]

Yet Jesus rescues them. He does not command them to believe before he rescues them. He responds to their unbelieving cry for help. So, unlike most other miracle stories in the Gospels, this is a miracle performed, not in response to the beneficiaries' faith, but in spite of its absence.

---

[4] Luke (4.42) changes both subject and verb ("the crowds came looking for him").

[5] Particularly striking is the Marcan irony in the emphatic position of *pantes* at 14.23 and 14.50: "they drank from it (sc. the cup) – *all of them*" and "they ran away – *all of them*".

[6] A transliteration of Mark's expression for "unbelieving generation".

[7] Marshall, op. cit. pp. 223-24.

[8] Commentators often compare the story of Jonah, especially Jonah 1.6. Contrast the more polite words of the disciples in Matt 8.25 and Luke 8.24.

What does the canonical status of this story mean? In recognizing a document's canonical status, the Church was *ipso facto* acknowledging that its significance transcended its original life-setting. This means, for example, that we may expect to find, again and again, churches like Corinth, compromised by the prevailing culture, or churches like Galatia, imposing or accepting illegitimate admission requirements on "outsiders". Applied to this story, that must mean: disciples who behave like this are a recurring feature of Christian history. To put it another way, unbelieving believers will always need rescuing.

Two points of a general kind about the nature of faith need to be made at this point. Faith in God is not a simple or straightforward matter. Whatever people might say in response to a questionnaire, it cannot be reduced to a simple either/or: either we believe in God, or we do not. First, faith in the New Testament is a multi-dimensional word. The Greek word *pistis* can mean not only faith in the sense of believing trust, or trustful belief, but also loyalty and faithfulness. It therefore implies commitment and obedience, an idea most clearly expressed in Paul's phrase "the obedience of faith" (*hypakoen pisteos*, Rom 1.5). But this story implies yet another dimension of faith. Jesus' question to the disciples, "Why are you cowardly?" (v. 40a) suggests that the opposite of faith is cowardice.[9] So, secondly, belief in anything, if deeply held, will have practical outcomes. Richard Niebuhr's writings on God and on faith will help to elucidate the point. Niebuhr observes, rightly I think, that human beings are naturally polytheists The observation follows from his definitions of the words "faith" and "god":

> ... we cannot live without a cause, without some object of devotion, some centre of worth, something on which we rely for our meaning. In this sense all men (*sic*) have faith....

and:

> ... when we believe that life is worth living by the same act we refer to some being which makes our life worth living.... And this being, whatever it is, is properly termed our god...

Luther expressed this idea long ago:

> Whatever then thy heard clings to ... and relies upon, that is properly thy god.[10]

---

[9] Thus Catherine Keller, *Face of the Deep*, London: Routledge, 2003, p. 214.

[10] H.R. Niebuhr, *Radical Monotheism and Western Culture*, London: Faber and Faber, 1960, pp. 119f.

So the New Testament as a whole, and more recent theological reflection confirm the dynamic, multi-dimensional character of faith
implied in Mark's narrative.

In interpreting the Marcan story for today, it will be important to
avoid "forced relevance" and *parallelomania*, once criticised by Krister
Stendahl and Samuel Sandmel respectively. With that caveat we look
once again at Mark's narrative. One commentator has correctly observed that the storm was a "killer",[11] and interpreters have naturally
noted the value of this story to the early Christians "buffeted by waves
of persecution and suffering".[12] But the imagery of this story, together
with the political resonances of Mark's narrative, invite other interpretations, too.

First, the imagery of sea, wind and waves. The associations in the
Old Testament of watery chaos with anti-creation, and therefore anti-
God forces, are very clear:

> "You rule the raging of the sea;
> when its waves rise, you still them.
> You crushed Rahab like a carcass;
> you scattered your enemies with your mighty arm" (Ps 89.9–10)

The language of Psalm 69 makes even clearer the deathly associations of "the waters":

> "Save me, O God, for the waters have come up to my neck.
> I sink in deep mire …
> I have come into deep waters, and the flood sweeps over me".[13]

To a Christian audience, familiar with this biblical background, and
believing in a risen Christ, this story would be an anticipation of the
resurrection: a dramatic demonstration of God's power over the forces
of death. The forces of death, however, are not be identified *tout simple*
with, or located at, the end of biological life, as biblical writers knew
full well. These forces dominated and impoverished human life in,
sometimes, all-pervasive and crushing ways. This brings us to the political resonances of Mark's narrative.

A number of commentators – notably Ched Myers, Richard Horsley
and Christopher Rowland – have argued for a politically-edged understanding of New Testament writings such as Mark. Most recently,
writing in this interpretative tradition, Wilf Wilde identifies what he

---

[11] Richard I. Deibert, *Mark. Interpretation Bible Studies.* Geneva Press, Louisville,
1998, pp 46-48.

[12] So e.g. D.E. Nineham, *Saint Mark*, Pelican Gospel Commentaries, 1963, p. 147.

[13] The associations of the imagery with death are recognised, for example, by R.
Davidson, *The Vitality of Worship,* Grand Rapids: Eerdmans 1998, p. 217, and A. Cur-
tis, *Psalms,* London: Epworth, 2004, p. 144.

believes to be the political resonances of, for example, Mark 4, suggesting that the contemporary equivalent of the Roman Empire is "global capitalism".[14] Before such an interpretation is dismissed as far-fetched, or an example of over-heated apocalyptic, it is worth noting that the evangelist in this story attributes to Jesus the same command with which he ordered a demon to come out of the man in the synagogue, (literally, "be muzzled"; compare 1.25 and 4.39). This suggests that the (demonic) deathly force that oppressed the possessed man is identical with the lethal power of the storm.[15]

Two particular characteristics of contemporary global capitalism, in my view, justify the equation made by Wilde which, I am suggesting, is applicable to the story of the stilling of the storm. First, there is the inexorable drive in contemporary capitalism towards expansion and growth: expansion of business, and growth in production, spending, consuming and profits. There are two problems about this relentless growth: one is spiritual, the other physical. The spiritual problem is encapsulated in a seldom noticed equation made by Paul (or deutero-Paul) in Col 3.5: ... *ten pleonexia hetis estin eidololatria*: the desire for more is idolatry. The physical problem which accompanies this unbridled *pleonexia* is, as we are becoming increasingly aware, the environmental degradation which threatens to become catastrophic in its consequences.

But there is a second major problem with contemporary global capitalism, and that is the injustice which accompanies it. How far the World Bank and the IMF – and with them the neo-conservative views which have dominated them for several decades now – are responsible for this is for others to determine. What is undeniable is that a major consequence of contemporary capitalism has been, not only a growing gap between rich and poor, but increasing wealth gained, to some extent, at the expense of the poor.

For all these reasons I am suggesting that there is a "killer storm" raging amongst us, all the more lethal because its potential consequences have not been sufficiently acknowledged, not even in the churches. The poor of the world will need no persuading of the demonic (or at least malign) deathly power of this capitalism. Evidence of it is all around them. But what of those of us in the still largely affluent North? It could be argued that, unlike the disciples in the Markan story, we sleep, oblivious of our Lord's call to wake – while the ship

---

[14] W. Wilde, "Crossing the River of Fire", in *Mark's Gospel and Global Capitalism*, London: Epworth, 2006, pp. 235ff.

[15] R.T. France, however, in *The Gospel of Mark*, NIGTC, Grand Rapids: Eerdmans, 2002, p. 224, believes that this is "a lot to build on two verbs".

sails on to oblivion. We are, of course, becoming increasingly aware of the growing danger of self-destruction by the reckless exploitation of the planet. Whether we shall discover – or be given – the far-reaching *metanoia* to avert this catastrophe remains to be seen. But there is another potential consequence of this "killer storm", all the more dangerous because unnoticed or insufficiently acknowledged, and that is a kind of spiritual asphyxiation.

In the early 1980s a British Methodist returned from what was then a poverty-stricken Poland, observing that "we just do not see what our affluence is doing to us". To take that remark seriously is not to subscribe to an Ebionite gospel which proclaims that we are justified by our poverty. Nor does it mean ignoring the many creation-affirming texts of the Bible, mainly, but not only, in the Old Testament; for example, the writer of 1 Timothy refers to the "God who richly provides us with everything for our enjoyment" (6.17). It is, however, to take seriously the many dire warnings of the New Testament about the dangers of wealth, and the warnings of Old and New Testament alike that wealth won at the expense of the poor is abhorrent to God. So it should not surprise us if the same demonic power threatens rich and poor alike, even though in different ways, and even though the rich cannot see it.

We need to understand more deeply the biblical themes of judgement. (Liberal Christians tend to dismiss this, whilst conservatives are in danger of making it incredible by an over-literalist interpretation). First, Richard Niebuhr again: salvation, he writes, sometimes appears "in its harsher forms as judgement and discipline that re-order a world of disloyalties".[16] Second, Old and New Testaments alike testify to what Klaus Koch has called human action taking place "in an arena of built-in consequences set in motion, speeded up and finally brought to completion by Yahweh's active involvement".[17] Paul's language in Romans 1.18–32 is a clear example of the inter-action of human waywardness and divine judgement in the threefold use of *metellaxan*, "exchanged" (predicated of human action, for example, in exchanging the true worship of God for idolatry) and *paredoken*, "handed over" (predicated of divine action, in handing over humankind to experience the consequences of wrongdoing). Two such consequences are alluded to many times in the Bible: a "hardened heart" and a "darkened mind".

We seem to have travelled a long way from Mark's story. Yet have we? I am contending that we in the so-called developed world are like

---

[16] Niebuhr, op. cit., p. 43.

[17] Quoted in N. Richardson, *Paul's Language about God*, Sheffield: Sheffield Academic Press, 1994, p. 112. Cf. S. Schechther's concept of "measure for measure", discussed on p. 223.

the disciples in the story: we have embarked upon a lake where a killer storm is imminent or raging. If the storm took the form of severe personal affliction or overt persecution, we should have cried out to the Lord long ago. But because it results in slow spiritual asphyxiation in the form of hardened hearts and darkened minds, we may not notice it so readily. ("We just do not realise what our affluence is doing to us.")

Is this too severe a verdict? I do not write as one who is not enmeshed in, compromised by, and also a beneficiary of contemporary global capitalism. Nor am I suggesting that there are simple solutions to the increasingly dire situation in which we find ourselves. But I *am* suggesting, for example, that "the storm" is killing off the Church by individualizing and privatizing faith, by turning worshippers into consumers and worship into entertainment; by numbing our sensitivity to the obscenity of relegating deaths in faraway places (whether from earthquakes or war), to the inside pages of most newspapers or to the fourth item on television news bulletins, in deference to the latest change in domestic house prices, or the latest rise in energy and fuel prices.

There are more subtle ways in which the storm is wreaking spiritual havoc, but, again, biblical texts about judgement may alert us to what is happening. The NRSV translates Psalm 39.11:

> You chastise mortals in punishment for sin,
> consuming like a moth what is dear to them.

The precise meaning of the original is uncertain, but the verse seems to stand in the biblical tradition which recognised that our very sins and failings become our punishment (v. 16). For example, one of the things dear to most people in the developed world is time; time is money, or when time is leisure, we are spoilt for choice about what to pack into it, and, always, whether we are at work or at leisure, time is insufficient. Somehow, the time which is so dear to us is "consumed like a moth";[18] it is not unrelated to the increasing incidence of stress and depression.

But what of "the rescue of unbelieving believers" which, I have suggested, is a major theme of the Markan story? First, it is a story about the rescue of *disciples*. Jesus had said to them, "Let us go across to the other side" (v. 35b). So the disciples wouldn't have been on the lake at all if it had not been for Jesus. At first sight, this point may seem to tell against the interpretation I am offering here. But I think not.

---

[18] David Ford has written interestingly about the contemporary "container" view of time in *The Shape of Living*, London: Fount, 1997, chapter 5, "Leisure and Work – Shaping Time and Energy", pp. 107-36.

Disciples are called into the world, and so they are not exempt from its storms. So this story cannot mean that disciples will, by some "rapture-like" event, be spared, for example, the consequences of climate change. (The Markan apocalypse of chapter 13 suggests that they, along with everyone else, experience the crises of "the last days"). The issue, rather, is whether they will escape the spiritual death threatened by the storm.

The Markan story is a vivid enactment of the promise of Matthew 16.18:

> "the gates of Hades will not prevail against it (sc. my church)".[19]

The chaotic, demonic forces which the storm represents are silenced by Christ. Therefore the particular fate which threatens the disciples *qua* disciples can be avoided. Disciples will share with the world at large the tribulations of "the last days" but, as disciples, they will survive because the Lord of the storm will ensure that it will not reach their souls. So the Church is promised, not exemption from the storms of life and the world either then or now, but, as a community of disciples calling on their Lord even in unbelief, salvation as a Church chosen by Christ to be his disciples in the world.

Is the Church, then, indestructible? What is the promise here? It is simply this: the storm will not destroy you; that is, the power of evil, the anti-creation forces of chaos will not overwhelm you.[20] This does not mean that the Church cannot go a long way down the road of self-destruction; it has done so many times, and will likely do so again. It does not mean that the forces of evil will not win temporary or local "victories"; there are plenty of examples in the New Testament (e.g. Acts 8.1 and 12.1–2). It does not mean that God underwrites all our ways of being church. But the story does mean that a church which, even in its unbelief, cries out to God, will not be overcome. "Just as in his first word our Lord said, with his blessed passion in mind, "In this way is the devil overcome", so now in this last word he says with complete assurance – and he means us all – 'You will not be overcome'."[21]

It is time to return to the phrase, borrowed from Marshall's monograph, *Faith as a Theme in Mark's Narrative,* with which we began. The evangelist is both serious and realistic in portraying disciples as unbelieving. They had seen individuals healed, but a cosmic force in the form of a killer storm was another matter. Similarly, many of us today

---

[19] W.D. Davies and Dale C. Allison, *Matthew. A Shorter Commentary,* T. & T. Clark, 2004, pp. 269-70, see a clear connection between the Markan story and Matthew 16.16-18.

[20] On the word "overwhelming", see Ford, op. cit., especially pp. xiii-xxviii, 6-9.

[21] Julian of Norwich, *Revelations of Divine Love,* c. 20.

witness personal conversions and the like, but are faithlessly fatalistic about the principalities and powers which appear to dominate our world. This is why we cannot call Christian faith mature if it lacks the courage to challenge these powers.

Yet there is a serious danger — and that is not an over-statement — that the analogy between unbelieving believers then and now may break down at one vital point. In the Markan story it is the Lord who is asleep, the disciples in panic-stricken wakefulness. Today the Church is in danger of slumbering, of not being alert to the insistent command, "Keep awake".[22]

But we must end where Mark ends his Gospel — and I assume it was at 16.8. For years scholars have debated whether, or how far, Mark's theology is Pauline. Yet Mark 16.7 seems to be a remarkable example of one of Paul's most daring statements:

> … where sin increased, grace abounded all the more. (Rom 5.20b)

We observed at the beginning of this study that the nearer Jesus comes to his cross, the worse the disciples become, finally deserting him (14.50), and, in Peter's case, denying him (14.66–72). Yet, even though they have failed abysmally to keep their promises to him (14.29–31), Jesus keeps his promise to them (14.28; 16.7). So, in the end, there is hope even for unbelieving, faithless believers — provided they are brought to realise how desperate their plight is. There is no cheap grace on offer in the New Testament — only grace on the far side, so to speak, of a cross. Mark's story of the stilling of the storm, almost uniquely,,[23] proclaims grace for unbelieving believers.

---

[22] "Keep awake" is perhaps the most frequent command in the New Testament, after the commands to love and to "fear not".

[23] But note also the plea of the father of the epileptic boy in Mark 9.24: "I believe; help my unbelief!" This *cri de coeur* epitomises much of what Mark has to say about discipleship. In Morna Hooker's words (op. cit., p. 224), "He is the typical disciple".

8

Pushing the Boat Out for Mission and Ministry

LOUISE J. LAWRENCE

He said to them "Let us go across to the other side." And leaving the crowd behind they took him with them in the boat, just as he was. (Mark 4.36)

Like many peninsulas the "south west", has often been imagined as a "border place" surrounded by sea on three sides, its western most point known simply as "Land's End". Sea shores, though, do not just mark ends but also beginnings. It is from the edge of the shore that new horizons can be encountered. It is perhaps for this reason that we speak today of standing "on shore's edge" when responding to new and difficult challenges.

The story of the stilling of the storm also tells of a border place, a journey from a shore across Lake Galilee to Gentile territory beyond. This story as will be seen, can act as a powerful commentary on the collective identity and vision of 21st-century Christian communities, who may sense a variety of "storms" rocking the boat, but are still called to undertake a journey of discovery and transformation. Here I will briefly document contextual reflections on the Stilling of the Storm in light of the Diocese of Exeter's recent strategy, *Moving on in Mission and Ministry* (*MOIMM*),[1] which encourages parishes to work collaboratively to strengthen community resources for mission within their contexts. *MOIMM* still affirms the ecclesiastical parish system but encourages networks to be developed with a diversity of human communities (education; leisure; workplace) in order to allow the church to develop fullness of life within the local community. It is a strategy which attempts to deal seriously with the changing sense of place

---

[1] Documents on the *MOIMM* initiative are available online at http://www.exeter. anglican.org.

which has occurred throughout the western industrialised world, but affirmably is a plan for growth rather than the management of decline in church communities.

1. A Changing Sense of "Place"

From birth to death we humans are placed, but whilst in the past many communities were fairly static, born, working and worshipping in one place, eating locally produced crops, enjoying a network of support from fellow residents and at the last being buried with kin in the local graveyard, things are not the same today. Many of us travel far from our place of birth for education, work and leisure. Many others of us connect with global networks through the internet or more alarmingly with others in the same room by e-mail! The development of the "global village" have not come without a price on the local level, often "displacing" people, if not physically certainly psychologically, from their immediate contexts and neighbours. The very notion of "commuter villages" and "dormitory towns" speak of increasingly transitory ways of living. In the words of one commentator: "we have since the Second World War de-emphasised place for the sake of values such as mobility, centralisation" and economic gain (Sheldrake, 2001, p. 8). As a result,

> While for some the world is more compressed and globalized, for others it is increasingly lonely and fractious... The city may be alive and well with everything in easy reach, yet pensioners can still be living in bed-sits their presence or absence going undetected for months. In other words, the mobility of some, while destroying the identity of the 'local' for many, can equally leave many others depending even more heavily on their immediate environment and community for support. (Percy, 2006, p. 9)

It is not an unconnected point that the most popular social networking sites on the internet are called *My Space* and *Facebook* but never involve any embodied, personal, face-to-face interaction at all. You can be "virtually" anyone.

Over the last couple of decades as a result of these social trends, there has been a marked interest in "places" which are defined as having a shared community story and "a sense of belonging" fostered through close (often face to face) relationships. These "places" are often contrasted with their direct opposite, "non-places", which do not contain or promote the construction of shared stories. People can operate within them alone and anonymously. Supermarkets, airport lounges, chain-dominated high streets can denote this sort of "non-place" where one can become de-sensitised to the importance of bonds of relationships, histories and experiences with others in the same location (see Auge, 1995). The rise of "non-place" has also changed local community life. When communities don't communicate, not only is a rich vein of experience left un-mined (an old saying in Africa goes "when a person dies a library burns down") they also literally forget who they collectively are. The world is increasingly suffering from this corporate amnesia and does so at its peril.

2. A Changing Sense of Parish

If we are not placed in the way that communities, even a couple of generations ago were, then neither are we hefted in the way that the parish system originally envisaged. This model depended on the collective story of a community and their locality. The parish church provided a key focus for the residents and marked important personal and social occasions: it baptised children and was the place for the living to celebrate the community's departed. Graveyards surrounding the church were visible inscriptions of the circle of relationships both past and present, and a reminder of the inevitable circle of life and death. It is not without good reason that graveyards have accordingly been referred to as "the open books" of the community; yet increasingly cemeteries are now situated on the outskirts of a town (Percy, 2006, pp. 3-15).

In this respect is it any accident that etymologically the word "cemetery" does not even denote death but rather a "dormitory" or "sleeping place"? (Francis *et al.*, 2005, p. xvii). Could this be further evidence of a move away from "placing" the dead among the living, and a move towards a trend, symptomatic of the Western world's anaesthetising to the realities of corporeal existence and its dissolution, a "placing apart" of elements held to "hold [a] powerful and disturbing charge that is not comfortably resisted" (Francis *et al.*, 2005, p. 215). In a related vein, whilst church space was often perceived as community space used as a venue for debates, celebrations, get-togethers – constituting a "community comfort zone" in all its senses – for many outside, it is now perceived as the exclusive space of the worshipping community (Percy, 2006, pp. 3-15).

In a rural parish in Dartmoor it was no coincidence that the "place" the community said they would give up everything to retain was the local shop, not the parish church. The shop was where personal conversations took place and neighbourly concern was demonstrated on a day to day level. In light of this, one can only wonder at the wisdom and foresight of another community's move to physically situate the Post Office within the Church building, thus physically erasing a division between church and the local community. The changing state of place therefore also inevitably constitutes an uncertain time for the ecclesiastical parish model.

3. The Church: Fishing Trawler or Passenger Ferry?

All this talk of dislocation, place and non-place brings to mind themes encountered in the gospel narrative of the Stilling of the Storm and the Exorcism of Legion which directly follows it (Mk 4.35–5.20). Whilst these are often divided into two separate narratives (and chapters) it is clear from the gospel that the two complexes are related. The image of the "stirring up" is mirrored in the stormy sea and in the reaction of the people to Jesus after Legion's exorcism in the Gerasene area. More simply, the two episodes are framed as a journey to the other side and back again (5.21). The disciples are disorientated not only by the storm encountered *en route*, but also by their destination being marked by unclean tombs and pigs, all abhorrent to law-observant Jews.

Ultimately however, the story teaches that the disciples were purposefully called out from the familiarity of home not only to encounter another world but also to found a new people. Jesus knows "that places on the edge, those considered God-forsaken by many, are where his identity as Messiah has to be revealed … ever dragging his disciples away from the familiarity of home, he declares present the power of the kingdom in the alien landscapes of another land" (Lane, 1998, p. 46). They literally "pushed the boat out" for this purpose. We often use the phrase "pushing the boat out" today to denote those occasions when we spend more than we would normally do or when we a special occasion or turning point. In this story, the high point must be the liberation of Legion, the demon-possessed Gentile, who when released from his demonic torment goes around the Decapolis and declares how much God has done on his behalf through Jesus (Mk 5.20). Through this image Mark reminds his readers that the people of God includes those individuals that society may well conceive of as "out of place" in one way or another, including those "restrained with shackles and chains" (Mk 5.4).

The church throughout the ages has been pictured as a boat traversing the waves of adversity. Seas, storms and demons are often used within the biblical tradition to symbolise chaos and evil. Art and architecture throughout Christian history from the early Christian catacombs in Rome, right up to present day imaging of the "nave" (the Latin word for "ship" from whence we get the word "navy") testify to the understanding that "the world is a sea in which the Church, like a ship, is beaten by the waves, but not submerged" (Sil, 1996, p. 134). These waves may have changed in substance across the centuries, but can always be relied upon to "rock the boat" and demand action and faith to quell the storm. Picking up on the naval/ecclesial metaphor, Steven Croft in his recent book on the changing face of parishes urges Christian communities not to see such threats and storms as insurmountable, but urges them to take seriously the realities of the contexts in which thy operate. He writes:

> I see a Church that is beset by anxiety about the future ... fed by an almost continual blizzard of prophecies of doom and decline. We need to make wise decisions in order to shape our future ... our decisions need to be guided, tested and shaped by scripture. In a storm the boat needs its keel perhaps more than its rudder. Our decisions also need to be informed by the realities of the world in which we find ourselves. (Croft, 2006, p. viii)

If he is right that in storms the boat's keel is more important than its rudder, is it also true that the role of every crew member is also paramount? The one steering the boat cannot operate alone. In Mark's account no indication of the size or number of crew on the boat is given. The story also leaves the ownership of the boat open on the narrative level. Historians suggest that in Galilee boats were small and contracted from a boat owner on the understanding that they would be returned safely and unscathed (Keener, 1999, p. 278).

During my work within a Cornish fishing community, I learnt that likewise most fishing trawlers here in the South West are owned by a kin group or co-operative, but more usually hired out from a boat owner. The relationships between the crew members and the "Teacher" sleeping can also be understood more powerfully within a fishing community. Jesus asks about the crew's faith which the fishermen effectively interpreted as "Grow up. I am asleep. You do it!" Cross-cultural studies of fishing crews have time and again noted the egalitarian nature of relationships within the boat. This, it is proposed, is in part related to the need for skilled hands to face perilous dangers. In such situations the gap between crew and captain necessarily becomes much smaller. Acheson in his study of cross-cultural fishing practices likewise notes:

> ... The ideal skipper-crew relationship is one where crewmen remarked of the skipper "he's so quiet you hardly know the man is up there" or "he hardly says a word, and orders rarely have to be given". (Acheson, 1981, p. 279)

This co-operative system, based on equality of relationship, also has profound lessons to teach the "crew" of the church. New ways of being church and new developments within church structures, such as *MOIMM*, which have stressed the point that the gifts of all members of human communities ("liturgically, pastorally, administratively, educationally etc.") need to be used and capitalized on within local contexts, for this is the only way in which the abundance of the church's life can be communicated on the local level.

This was echoed in responses from a rural community in Dartmoor who, while bemoaning the fact that their rector was no longer resident in the village, nevertheless saw that this had led to the empowerment of others to take on ministry in all its forms within their context. Due to the changing nature of "place" the "crew" really does need to be envisaged in a much wider sense than just stipendary priests. Lay led initiatives need to be encouraged and developed. Likewise any collective movements in the locality which support or regenerate community also need to be supported by the church. Rowan Williams, writing at the turn of the millennium, likewise urged Christians to concern themselves "as best they can in those enterprises in their culture that seek to create or recover a sense of shared discourse and common purpose in human society" (Williams, 2000, p. 37). If the "all hands to deck" ethos is not promoted, the church becomes less a missionary-led fishing trawler with a proactive crew and more a passenger ferry with passive travellers. Such ships are heavy and hard to handle, difficult to get on board, and ill equipped to reach those at sea-level within a storm.

One of the most frequent misunderstandings about such strategies as *MOIMM* is that in the joining-up of Christian communities into coalitions for mission, in some way a church is being "displaced" from the local. Quite the contrary, in uniting and sharing wisdom together one is enabled, like the disciples and Legion, to return home, to the local, galvanised for future action. The journey encountered may involve symptoms sometimes resembling sea-sickness, but like the disciples and Legion, one returns to the local area transformed and reformed. A recent translation of John 1.14 more usually read as "the word of God pitched his tent among us" now declares "the word of God moved into the neighbourhood" to stress this very point. One particular church I worked with had physically changed the church into a community space which offered everything from dancing, pottery, shelter, to computer lessons. The association of the "journey to the other side" with the intent to found a new people encapsulated for this community the concept of "sanctuary" far better than the former church building did as the "exclusive" place of the church community. Now the young, the elderly as well as performers, artists and creative thinkers, all have a stake in the activities within the centre. We have to re-imagine the crew in this 21st-century Western context. The church needs to think deeply about its part in "place-making" in contemporary culture. Percy incisively makes that point that it is no accident that the word "Parish" actually never appears in scripture; it derives from a term which originally referred to those areas of cities within the Roman Empire where non-citizens lived (see Percy, 2006). "Parish" thus referred to the "outsiders" rather than the "insiders". Archbishop William Temple famously said that the church was the only club which existed for non-members. Thus the crew of the boat likewise should be radically re-imagined along those terms. *MOIMM* in a similar spirit urges communities in the Diocese of Exeter to reflect on the network of human communities they inhabit (in education, work, leisure and not just "the church") and encourages them to develop in these assorted contexts touchstones of the kingdom of God. The marks of the church's fullness of life on a local level are identified by *MOIMM* as worship; prayer; pastoral care; evangelisation; learning and teaching opportunities; nurture for disciples of all ages; youth and children's work and worship; equipping members for ministry in the community and local church; connecting with the local community especially in service to the poor (*MOIMM*, p. 9). All these are not the sole domain of the parish church but rather can be pursued in a variety of local contexts.

4. Pushing the Boat Out: A Powerful Vision for Change

Unpredictable powers and their consequent threat to human flourishing were themes in the story of the Stilling of the Storm which are readily transplanted and adopted into the context of *MOIMM* and similar church strategies to deal with changing cultural waters. Like all biblical narratives this story is ever old and ever new. Like the crew who were fearful for their lives on a storm-ravaged lake Galilee, "the boat", "the journey to the other side", "the sea and storm" and "the crew" can provide powerful commentaries not only on present situations but also offer powerful resources to envision the future as demonstrated in the *MOIMM* scheme. While sometimes it seems as if we stand precariously on "the edge of the shore" new horizons often give clearer views of where we should be heading and also transformed views of where we return to.

Bibliography

Augé, M., *Non-Places: Introduction to an Anthropology of Supermodernity* [tr. J. Rowe], London: Verso, 1995 [original 1992].

Acheson, J.M., "Anthropology of Fishing", *Annual Review of Anthropology* 10 (1981), pp. 275-316.

Bird, S.E., "It Makes Sense to Us: Cultural Identity in Local Legends of Place", *Journal of Contemporary Ethnography* (2002), pp. 519-47.

Croft, S., ed., *Explorations: The Future of the Parish System: Shaping the Church of England in the 21st Century*, Church House Publishing, 2006, pp. 3-15.

Edmondson, C. and E. Ineson, eds., *Celebrating Community: God's Gift for Today's World*, London: Darton, Longman and Todd, 2006.

Edson, M., "Community and Conflict" in C. Edmondson and E. Ineson, eds., pp. 111-26.

Francis, D., L. Kellaher, and G. Neophytou, *The Secret Cemetery*, Berg, 2005.

Keener, C., *A Commentary on the Gospel of Matthew*, Grand Rapids: Eerdmans, 1999.

Lane, B., *The Solace of Fierce Landscapes*, Oxford: Oxford University Press, 1998.

Lawrence, L.J., "Being Hefted: Reflections on Place, Stories and Contextual Bible Study", *Expository Times* 118, 2007a, pp. 530-35.

—— , "On a Cliff's Edge: Actualizing Luke 8.22-39 in an Intentional Christian Community on the North Devon Coast", *Expository Times* 119, 2007b, pp. 111-15.

—— , "The Stilling of the Sea and the Imagination of Place in a Cornish Fishing Village", *Expository Times* 120.4, January 2009, pp. 172-77.

Macintyre, B., "Are You Hefted? If Not That's a Pity", *The Times* (2007) available online at www.timesonline.co.uk.

Moore, S., "Mark and Empire: Zealot and Postcolonial Readings" in R.S. Sugirtharajah, ed., *The Postcolonial Biblical Reader*, Oxford: Blackwell Publishing, 2006, pp. 193-205.

Moxnes, H., *Putting Jesus in His Place: A Radical Vision of Household and Kingdom*, Louisville: Westminster John Knox, 2003.

Percy, M., "Many Rooms in my Father's House: The Changing Identity of the English Parish Church", in S. Croft, ed., pp. 3-15.

Sheldrake, P., *Spaces for the Sacred: Place, Memory and Identity*, Baltimore: Johns Hopkins University Press, 2001.

Sil, G., *A Handbook of Symbols in Christian Art*, Austin: Touchstone, 1996.

West, G., *The Academy of the Poor: Toward a Dialogical Reading of the Bible*, Sheffield: Sheffield Academic Press, 1999.

Reports

Moving on in Mission and Ministry Report available online at: http://www.exeter.anglican.org.

9

An Inner-City "Other Side"

JOHN VINCENT

It's a story of getting over to "the other side". That is our problem as disciples – he wants to get there – "let's go", he says (4.35) and he will eventually succeed in doing so (5.1). It's another story of Jesus saying "Let's go" to his disciples, as he did in 1.38. We are the "us" that he constitutes and affirms. He doesn't go without disciples. In both 1.38 and 4.35, the crowd are left behind (1.37; 4.36), though we do not know who are in the "other boats" (4.36).

But the disciples have to take him. "Leaving the crowd behind, they (the disciples) took him with them in the boat", apparently without him being prepared for it – "just as he was". So that Jesus' *wish* to go to the other side is landed in the power of the disciples' provision. They provide the boat, and others (disciples also?) provide other boats also (4.36).

So Jesus is getting taken across the sea, over the demonic deep.[1] He can take it easy. He sleeps, calmly, on a cushion at the back of the boat (4.38). Getting him across is disciples' business. After all, aren't they fishermen? (1.16–20). Sailing boats is their calling. Jesus is the precious cargo to be transported. He has just told the people about the Kingdom of heaven on earth (4.1–32) and explained it to the disciples (4.10–12; 4.34). Now he wants to get the message "to the other side". All the disciples have to do is set sail and steer and row. Meantime, he can sleep, like the man in the parable (4.27). He has sown the Kingdom seeds (4.26) which then grow "automatically" (4.28). He can take it easy, now, sleeping on a cushion.

---

[1] Cf. Paul J. Achtemeier, "Person and Deed: Jesus and the Storm-Tossed Sea", *Interpretation* 16 (1962), pp. 169-76 – on wind and sea embodying demonic forces.

While Jesus sleeps, the disciples are the ones who have to get themselves ("let's all go," he says, 4.35) over to the other side.

This dramatic incident comes at the end of a day (4.35) in which Jesus has been trying to explain to the disciples what character and significance they are of. The truth is that they are people whose true character is being revealed by Jesus as their "teacher" (4.36) or, perhaps better, "Master" (Luke 8.24) or "Lord" (Matt 8.25). And what Jesus has been teaching them is that they, the disciples, have the precious seed of the Kingdom within them. The whole of chapter 4 has been about this, about how the precious seed in them now makes them precious:

24. Take heed what you hear
    The amount you can give out
    is the amount you receive
    (plus a bit extra)
25. For
    The person who has something
      will get more
    The person who has nothing
      will lose what he has(n't!)

All this is about the need for total concentration on the Kingdom and its mysteries. If you are into that, you can't afford to fill your head with other things. Especially because, when it comes to sharing the mystery (v. 24) you'll only be able to give out things that you have been given, or obtained (v. 24). So when it comes to Kingdom matters, if you have the key to the mystery (4.11), you will get more and more of the mystery.

The two parables which follow make this clear.

In 4.26–29, the Seed Growing Secretly is the secret of the Kingdom which, if not disrupted, will grow more and more, so that it will produce a harvest – the full-grown communicable Kingdom!

In 4.30–32, the Mustard Seed is the tiny secret of the Kingdom which, unless prevented, will grow up into the largest plant, which everyone will come and settle under – the full-grown communicable Kingdom!

It is the Twelve, in whom this vital seed of the Kingdom has been sown (4.11) who are now to be taken to the other side (4.35)! If only they can carry it across safely with them, all will be well – and Jesus can sleep!

But it's no good. There's a storm. It isn't a problem for him. Such trifling interferences are not significant, and can be quickly removed (4.39).

It's a problem for disciples, though. We are perishing (4.38), even if he is not. The question, "Why are you so cowardly?" perhaps recalls Deuteronomy 20.8, where the Greek word *deilos*, cowardly, describes the lack of battle-readiness in would-be soldiers. Disciples are involved, like Jesus, in a battle against evil forces, and must not cave in when the forces exert themselves.[2]

Disciples have to learn how to be faithful in storms. A Qumran writer describes himself as a sailor on a ship in the midst of furious seas, with waves and roaring billows (*Thanksgiving Hymns*, 1QH 14.22–24). When the mighty Counsellor appears, those who practice injustice will be like sailors whom the abyss will swallow up (1QH 11.9–18).[3]

As the disciples are now the bearers within them of the precious secret that the Kingdom is now present on earth, they must hold the seed safely within them, so that the Kingdom will appear more and more.

Hence, in the storm, they should have been able to act responsibly, bearers of the precious seed as they are, without waking Jesus up (4.36). Is it not God's seed now within them? Would not God then guard his seed, and thus them also? Have the disciples no trust in this, even though they have the Kingdom seed (4.40)?

It may be that, in the story, Jesus chides the disciples with their incompetence as miracle operators. So Ian Wallis:

> Jesus admonishes the disciples because they fail to demonstrate that kind of miracle-working faith which has power over the natural elements. He then replaces them in the role of miracle worker, stills the storm by exhibiting that faith which they lacked, and thereby provides the disciples and the early Church with another example of faith in action.[4]

So, it's about disciples getting to the "other side". Jesus and his disciples are the bearers of the reality of the Kingdom of heaven on earth, a beautiful mystery given to them (4.11), enshrined in parables which contain within them the seeds of the kingdom (4.3; 4.14; 4.26; 4.31), which absolutely without question will grow and come to fruition (4.8; 4.20; 4.29; 4.32), so that their sowers can ignore them (4.3; 4.14; 4.27; 4.31), and even sleep (4.27; 4.38).

And now?

---

[2] So Suzanne Watts Henderson, *Christology and Discipleship in the Gospel of Mark*. Cambridge: Cambridge University Press, 2006, p. 140.

[3] Cf. Adela Yarbro Collins, *Mark: A Commentary*, Hermeneia; Minneapolis, MN: Fortress, 2007, p. 259.

[4] Ian G. Wallis, *The Faith of Jesus Christ in Early Christian Traditions*, Cambridge: Cambridge University Press, 1995, p. 39.

Now, on our street, it's about our journey as would-be Kingdom bearers "going over to the other side" of contemporary urban society. It's about our "boat", a street-corner shop in inner city, deprived, multi-racial, multi-ethnic Burngreave, Sheffield.[5] It's about going with a frail, decrepit, dilapidated, rundown set of 1907 premises. And fancying that he, with all the mysteries of God's present Kingdom on earth, is the one we take with us in our "boat" (4.36). He is with us, as we are with him (3.14), trusting that the seed, if sown faithfully, can be relied upon to grow "automatically", of itself (4.28). And we, perhaps, are believing that the dynamic source of this ongoing inmundation might even awake (4.39) and take action if things really get too rough, and the waves of the sea (the drug sellers, the youths with guns, the gangs, the planners, the politicians, the principalities and powers, the world rulers of this darkness (Eph 6.12) lead us to cry "we are perishing".

At the beginning, in 2001, we called the Burngreave Ashram "a Sign of the Incarnation, and a Place where Kingdom of God things might happen".[6] In our context, we feel many points of affinity with the Twelve.[7] And even so far, there have been a few but significant "signs following" (16.17) in the midst of our journey in this boat to the other side.

First, a few other little boats are beginning to join us (4:36). The spectacle of apparently sane, committed, open, welcoming people, motivated by some inscrutable perversity, come to Spital Hill, seems to inspire others to brings their projects also.

Second, the storms have actually abated (4.39). The drug sellers, the youths with guns, and the gangs have moved elsewhere – which is good news at least for us.

Third, we are living by parables (4.34). We are seeing parables, like grains of wheat falling into the ground, or like mustard trees beginning to grow, or wheat and tares growing together.[8]

Fourth, as we become more and more exposed to and part of "the other side" (many faiths, regeneration initiatives, local politics, shopkeepers under threat), the more we feel at home in the other side (5.1), and wonder what it will make of us, or make us into.

---

[5] Cf. Eurig Scandrett, Helen Tomlinson and John Vincent, *Journeying with Ashram*. Sheffield: Ashram Press, 2005. pp. 15f, 20-22, 26f.

[6] In 2001, I reflected on the early months at Burngreave Ashram in the light of John 20.19-27 in "With Dirty Hands", *Bible and Practice*, ed. Christopher Rowland and John Vincent, Sheffield: Urban Theology Unit, 2001, pp. 100-11.

[7] Cf. John Vincent, "Outworkings: Twelve as Christian Community", *Expository Times*, September 2008, pp. 582-88.

[8] John Vincent, "Outworkings: Urban Mission in Mark 4", *Expository Times*, August 2011, pp. 531-38.

The incident of "an unclean spirit from among the tombs" suddenly coming up and taking the total attention of Jesus – and, presumably, the disciples (5.2), totally overcoming our Kingdom-bearing agenda with his violence and madness (5.3), so that no-one can control him (5.4), is not promising. We have seen his like on Spital Hill. He cannot be controlled by friends or authorities (5.3). He shouts endlessly (5.5). He harms himself (5.5). So, we ask with fear – From out of the *melée* of the inner city, who will come running to us and flinging themselves down and crying, "What do you want with me?" (5.7)?

And, for God's sake, there is a Legion of them (5.9)! And we are only twelve, plus him! And the "possessed man" is so committed to his present way of life, that he begs us to let him continue, even if it is "being possessed" (5.10).

Indeed, our inner city "other side" invites comparison with the Markan "other side" in a number of ways.

Christopher Burdon argues that Mark sees Jesus' crossing "to the other side" as "a paradigm of his own and the implied readers' continuing transition to engagement with the Other", in which, indeed, in our own culture, "the construction of the other specifically as Evil permits and justifies violence, exclusion and the refusal of repentance and change".[9] Yet this is understandable in Mark, since the early followers needed to be clear about "those inside" and "those outside" (cf. 4.11–12), and to characterise their group (in fact, a persecuted one) as good, and "those outside" as thus the opposition – as evil.[10]

Crossing the Sea of Galilee "to the other side" (*eis to peran*) occurs five times, in Mark 4.35, 5.1, 5.21, 6.45 and 8.13.

> When "the other side" is actually reached (and at 5.1 Mark repeats *eis to peran*) there is no doubt about its alienness. The symbols of non-Israelite uncleanness abound, in tombs and pigs and shackles and a pagan title for Jesus, all portrayed with considerable ribaldry. Here is an axis of evil, a land to be liberated…[11]

Jesus does "liberate" it, with Gentiles first running away (5.14), then failing to praise Jesus (5.15), and finally sending him away (5.17). Only the healed demoniac spreads the news in the Gentile ten cities (5.20). But Mark has more. The evil opposition reveal themselves as "Legion",

---

[9] Christopher Burdon, "To the Other Side: Construction of Evil and Fear of Liberation in Mark 5.1–20", *Journal for the Study of the New Testament* 27.2, 2004, pp. 149-67, p. 147.

[10] Burdon, p. 155.

[11] Burdon, p. 156.

that is, not only a Gentile but a Roman "principality and power",[12] who beg to remain in supportive Gentile territory (5.10), even though they are to be exterminated there (5.13).

The dramatic ambiguity of success and failure "on the other side" in fact in this story leads to a hasty retreat (5.18). The mission tackled a single oppressive factor, set loose a "good news" story. A single Gentile is now proclaiming "all that Jesus did for him" (5.20). But there is nothing more, at least at the time. So the disciples might well have wondered, Was it all in the end worth the agony of the journey over? If it is about "crossing boundaries", the conclusion is rather unclear for the disciples, and "the reader is no less puzzled than they are."[13]

Other "Gentile Mission" pieces in Mark end up rather puzzling. The non-children as dogs (7.24–30) is not an unambiguous call to or from Gentiles, and the feeding of the four thousand (8.1–10) only suggests Gentiles by its numbers. Jesus' own reference to "all the ethnic peoples" (13.10) refers to the future. Richard Horsley argues that "crossing to the other side" does not necessarily mean a Judean west and a Gentile east of Galilee.[14] In the main, Gentiles and Gentile areas in Mark are caught between Rome and Israel/Judea.[15]

The confusion confirms our confusion on Spital Hill. What it means to be Gospel people there emerges in fits and starts, in sudden happenings, in moves and developments that quickly get reversed. Perhaps the Gentile Mark tells the Galileans' story precisely because they, like us, know that it was all for "all the *ethnoi*", but also know that it gets messy whenever you really go over to another side and start doing things there. But you still go.

---

[12] With Ched Myers, *Binding the Strong Man: A Political Reading of Mark's Story of Jesus*, Maryknoll, NY: Orbis, 1988, pp. 31, 190-94.

[13] Bas van Iersel, *Mark: A Reader-Response Commentary*, Sheffield: Sheffield Academic Press, 1998, p. 193.

[14] Richard Horsley, *Hearing the Whole Story: The Politics of Plot in Mark's Gospel*, Louisville: Westminster John Knox Press, 2001, p. 46. Cf. also Burdon, pp.165-66.

[15] John Rogerson and John Vincent, *The City in Biblical Perspective*, London: Equinox, 2009, pp. 45-50.

10

Applying the SIFT Method

LESLIE FRANCIS

Introduction

A real strength in contemporary hermeneutics concerns the ways in which the context of the reader, the preacher, or the listener is taken seriously. Practice interpretation, as defined by Vincent (2006:3-32), shares this strength. Attempts to define and to understand context have properly led to the dynamic dialogue between biblical studies and modern sociology. The very invention of the Institute for Socio-Biblical Studies attests to the seriousness with which such dialogue is taken. No serious understanding of the contemporary contexts in which scriptures are proclaimed, interpreted and applied is now adequate without reference to theories, methods and data generated within the disciplines of sociology.

More recently there has developed alongside this increasingly established dialogue between biblical studies and modern sociology an equally important parallel dialogue between biblical studies and modern psychology. Such dialogue provides a different but equally important set of insights into the context within which scripture is being read, interpreted, proclaimed, heard and applied. In this sense, contemporary hermeneutics becomes concerned with psychological perspectives on individuals and on groups of individuals as much as with sociological perspectives on context. Practice interpretation is well placed to take these psychological perspectives as seriously as the sociological perspectives.

The SIFT method of biblical hermeneutics and liturgical preaching, shaped by Francis (2003, 2006) and applied by Francis and Atkins (2000, 2001, 2002), provides a stimulating example of the kind of contribution that can be made by modern psychology to biblical studies. Theologically, the SIFT method is rooted in the dominical command to love the Lord your God not only with all your heart, with all your soul and with all your strength, but also with all your mind (Mark 12.29–30). Psychologically, the SIFT method is rooted in Carl Jung's model of the human mind (Jung, 1971). This model, known as psychological type, has been expanded and developed by instruments like the Myers-Briggs Type Indicator (Myers and McCaulley, 1985) and the Keirsey Temperament Sorter (Keirsey and Bates, 1978), and has been widely applied within the Christian community through books like *God's Diverse People* (Osborn and Osborn, 1991), *Knowing Me Knowing You* (Goldsmith and Wharton, 1993), *Pray Your Way* (Duncan, 1993), and *Faith and Psychology* (Francis, 2005).

At heart, the theory of psychological type distinguishes between two mental processes: the perceiving process is concerned with gathering information and the judging process is concerned with evaluating information. Psychological type theory maintains that both these processes can be expressed through two contrasting functions. The two perceiving functions are defined as sensing (S) and intuition (N). The two judging functions are defined as thinking (T) and feeling (F). According to the theory each individual possesses an innate preference for one of the perceiving processes over the other (either S *or* N) and for one of the judging processes over the other (either T *or* F). As a consequence of such innate preferences the opposite function in each case is less preferred, less used, and less developed. The theory draws parallel with handedness, according to which most people seem innately to prefer either their right hand or their left hand, with the consequences that the less preferred hand becomes less well practiced and remains less well developed.

Moreover, according to the theory for each individual either the preferred perceiving function or the preferred judging function takes precedence over the other and emerges as the dominant function. It is the dominant function that often shapes an individual's recognised strengths. The practical person is shaped by dominant sensing, the imaginative person by dominant intuition, the humane person by dominant feeling and the logical person by dominant thinking. Such psychological type preferences also seem to relate to ways in which different individuals read, interpret and apply scripture. It is for this reason that psychological type theory may be so important for practice interpretation.

Two practical implications are drawn from psychology of type theory in the development of the SIFT method of biblical hermeneutics and liturgical preaching. First, it is recognised that psychological type preferences will both draw individuals to some particular perspectives on scripture and also blind them to other perspectives. Scripture as proclaimed by an intuitive preacher may seem particularly obscure to a dominant sensing listener, while scripture as proclaimed by a sensing preacher may seem particularly dull to a dominant intuitive listener. Second, if the command to love God with all the mind is taken seriously and if it is assumed that the full richness of scripture can only be appreciated by the complementary perspectives offered by all four psychological functions, then it becomes important to approach scripture in the disciplined way which permits all four functions to speak.

The SIFT method of biblical hermeneutics and liturgical preaching will now be applied to Mark 4.35–5.1, addressing the four functions of sensing, intuition, feeling and thinking in turn and in that order. In this case the application is offered in the service of practice interpretation.

Sensing

The sensing function is concerned with getting the information sorted out and with getting the facts lined up in a row. Practice interpretation could lose touch with the biblical text, if it failed to be properly grounded through the sensing function.

So become sensing people and make sure that you have put Mark 4.35–5.1 into context. As sensing people, hear the text, "On that day, when evening had come". Quite a lot has already taken place in the earlier verses of Mark's Gospel and you need to remember all that, before this passage makes sense.

Become sensing people and remember how Mark sets the scene as soon as John had been arrested (1.14–15). Jesus came "proclaiming the Gospel of God" and saying "the Kingdom of God is upon you". Already by the end of chapter 4 you have experienced three powerful signs of the presence of the Kingdom of God: the call of disciples, the restoration to wholeness, and the proclamation of the word.

Become sensing people and see the disciples called. See Simon Peter and his brother Andrew at work with a casting net; and see them leave their boat to follow Jesus. See John and his brother James overhauling their nets; and see them leave their boat to follow Jesus. See Levi at work in the custom-house; and see him leave his office to follow Jesus. See all twelve called and named. Open your eyes, for here is irrefutable evidence of God's reign.

Become sensing people and witness the restoration to wholeness. See the possessed man in the synagogue at Capernaum; and see the unclean spirit convulse the man and go. See the leper approach, kneel and beg for help; and see Jesus send him away cleansed. See the paralysed man let down through the roof on a stretcher; and see him pick up his stretcher and walk away whole. Open your eyes, for here is irrefutable evidence of God's reign.

Become sensing people and listen to the teaching. Hear about how the sower sowed seed, and how some brought forth a hundredfold. Hear about how the lamp is never placed under the meal-tub or under the bed, but on the lamp stand. Hear about how the mustard seed is the smallest of seeds at its sowing, but grows into the tallest of shrubs. Prick up your ears, for here is irrefutable evidence of God's reign.

Now with all this background you are ready to hear Jesus' call "Let us go across to the other side"; you are ready to get into the boat and to trust God's reign. Once in that boat become sensing people and savour fully the terror of the tempest.

> Hear the roaring wind whipped up all around you.
> See the rolling waves building up all over the lake.
> Feel the frail timbers of the boat rock and shake.
> Smell the danger in the air.
> Taste the terror in the boat.

Become sensing people and recognise that this is no ordinary everyday storm. Listen to the command "Peace! Be still!" and recognise that this is no ordinary everyday interaction with the forces of nature. Experience the great calm and newly-created order, and recognise that this is no ordinary everyday occurrence. Open your eyes, prick up your ears, for here is irrefutable evidence of God's reign.

Intuition

The intuitive function is concerned with grasping the possibilities, and with exploring the connections between one idea and another. Practice interpretation could fail to grasp the fullest implications of the biblical text, if it failed to be properly informed through the intuitive function.

So become intuitive people and make sure that you can forge the links between Mark 4.35–5.1 and what the Spirit is saying to you and to the churches today. As intuitive people, hear the text of invitation, "Let us go across to the other side". Here is a gospel that calls us to openness, to adventure and to change. Looked at that way, this is the dominant theme of all that has happened so far in Mark's Gospel.

Become intuitive people and revisit Jesus' call to Simon Peter. Here is the invitation to leave behind nets and boats; to leave behind a well-established way of life; to leave behind family and friends; to leave behind wife and mother-in-law. Here is a radical new beginning for personal lives, and the way ahead was by no means storm-free. So what aspects of your personal life is Jesus calling you to leave behind when he issues the call, "Let us go across to the other side"? And what storms will you confront on the way?

Become intuitive people and revisit Jesus' call to Levi. Here is the invitation to re-evaluate priorities; to re-evaluate a whole life style; to re-evaluate the value of a religious commitment once forsaken; to re-evaluate the role in life for wealth and personal gain. Here is a radical new beginning for social and religious values, and the way ahead was by no means storm free. So what among your values and priorities is Jesus calling you to re-evaluate when he issues the call, "Let us go across to the other side"? And what storms will you confront on the way?

Become intuitive people and revisit Jesus' interaction with the religious leaders of his day. Here is the invitation to re-assess how the Sabbath is used; to re-assess how healing and freedom can be offered; to re-assess how sinners can be welcomed and restored; to re-assess how forgiveness can be proclaimed and claimed. Here is a radical new beginning for religious faith, religious teaching, and religious law, and the way ahead was by no means storm-free. So what among your most dearly held and cherished beliefs is Jesus calling you to re-assess when he issues the call, "Let us go across to the other side"? And what storms will you confront on the way?

Feeling

The feeling function is concerned with what it is to be fully human and with the rich relational connections between individuals. Practice interpretation could fail to reflect the full gospel commitment to peace among people, to harmony in human living, and to the God of mercy, if it failed to give due weight to the feeling function.

So become feeling people and make sure that you can place yourselves in the shoes of the characters in the narrative of Mark 4.35–5.1. As feeling people, hear the text of heart-felt anguish, "Teacher, do you not care that we are perishing?" Here is a gospel that faces life as it really is and that tells the experience as it really wracks the human heart.

Become feeling people and experience how in the terror of the storm the disciples replayed their Christian experience. Jesus had disrupted personal lives when James and John left Zebedee behind in the boat, and when Simon left his wife and mother-in-law behind in the house. Was all this personal change to be lost in the storm; and who cares?

Jesus had disrupted professional lives when fishermen hung up their oars, and when a tax collector walked out of his office. Was all this professional change to be lost in the storm; and who cares?

Jesus had disrupted social lives when people from different walks of life were pressed together in the same boat, when the Zealot and the tax collector became companions in the Kingdom of God. Was all this social change to be lost in the storm; and who cares?

Jesus had disrupted belief systems when the teaching of the law was stood on its head, when the outcasts became accepted and when the righteous were pushed to the margins. Was all this religious change to be lost in the storm; and who cares?

Became feeling people and experience how in the terror of the storm the disciples recognised the rocky side of discipleship for what it truly is. They had been challenged by unclean spirits crying out in the synagogue. They had been challenged by the sick longing for healing. They had been challenged by teachers of the law debating forgiveness. They had been challenged by Pharisees because they had eaten with Levi, because they had plucked corn on the Sabbath, because their Lord was revealing the reign of God. Now even the elements, the wind and the water, were stirred up against them.

Do you not recognise points of your own Christian pilgrimage in that self-same boat, and do you not with them cry aloud, "Teacher, do you not care that we are perishing?"

Thinking

The thinking function is concerned with logic, with testing truth claims and with objectivity. Practice interpretation could fail to reflect the full gospel commitment to fairness among people, to truthfulness in human dealings, and to the God of justice, if it failed to give due weight to the thinking function.

So become thinking people and make sure that you can test the coherence, the logic and the theology of Mark 4.35–5.1. As thinking people, hear the text of profound theological importance, "Who is this, that even the wind and the sea obey him?" Here is a gospel that poses the ultimate and the fundamental question of the Christian faith.

Become thinking people and assess the evidence as it has been placed before you by Mark. The evidence is that he came into Galilee, proclaiming the gospel of God. So who could do that? The evidence is that he called new leaders for the twelve tribes of Israel (or thirteen, depending on what you make of Levi and of the Levites). So who could do that? The evidence is that he offers a new kind of teaching and does that with authority. So who could do that?

Become thinking people and assess the evidence as it has been placed before you by Mark. The evidence is that he is demonstrating the reign of God by exorcism and by healing. So who could do that? The evidence is that he is redefining the will of God by displaying release from sin and by liberalising the Sabbath. So who could do that? The evidence is that his authority stretches over the raging of the seas, the roaring of the winds, and the primordial forces of chaos. So who could do that?

Become thinking people, anticipate the question soon to be asked of the disciples, "Who do you say I am?"; and assess the adequacy of Peter's response, "You are the Messiah". Today people are asking that very same question; but do the old answers continue to suffice?

Conclusion

By taking Mark 4.35–5.1 as an applied example, this chapter has set out to test the thesis that the SIFT method of biblical hermeneutics and liturgical preaching could be of service to practice interpretation by focusing attention on what happens when the four distinctive voices of the Jungian functions (sensing, intuition, feeling and thinking) engage with the same passage of scripture. In this example, practice interpretation has been invited to step inside the biblical narrative (sensing), to engage with the gospel call for transformation (intuition), to experience and to accept the turbulence of discipleship (feeling), and to face the central Christological question of faith (thinking). In this sense, one passage speaks in diverse ways and fulfils its potential to engage with the beliefs, practices and daily lives of the people of God who are going about building and displaying the reign of God in their own highly contextualised situations.

The discipline that the SIFT method brings to practice interpretation may help to protect practice interpretation from a fundamental criticism which may be directed toward many applied or contextual approaches to scripture. The criticism is this. By employing scripture to illuminate specific practical situations, practice interpretation establishes a hermeneutical dialogue between the practical situation and the text in a way through which the practising believer anticipates revelatory insight. God speaks to the new situation through dialogue with the tradition. In such hermeneutical processes, the tradition must be allowed the potential for transformatory critique as well as for comforting support. The danger is that any partial dialogue, relying on one dominant voice or dominant psychological function, may eclipse the

full potential of the revelatory encounter. Practice interpretation becomes vulnerable, therefore, to the criticism that it may be using text
only selectivity to support particular viewpoints. Such misuse of scripture is all too well documented in other areas, as illustrated for example
by the recent psychological critique of fundamentalism proposed by
Hood, Hills and Williams (2005).

The hermeneutical process required by the SIFT method, however,
requires each preferred voice to be set alongside three other distinctive
voices to which equal revelatory authority needs to be given. Thus, for
example, the voice of conservatism preferred by the sensing function is
set systematically alongside the voice of innovation preferred by the
intuitive function, while the voice of mercy preferred by the feeling
function is set systematically alongside the voice of justice preferred by
the thinking function. In this way the dominical command to love the
Lord your God with all your mind may lead to a richer practice interpretation of scripture relevant to the specific situation and relevant to
the specific context.

References

Duncan, B., *Pray Your Way: Your Personality and God*, London: Darton,
    Longman and Todd, 1993.
Francis, L.J., 'Psychological Type and Biblical Hermeneutics: SIFT Method of
    Preaching' in *Rural Theology*, 1, 2003, pp. 13-23.
——, *Faith and Psychology: Personality, Religion and the Individual*, London:
    Darton, Longman and Todd, 2005.
——, 'Psychological Type and Liturgical Preaching: The SIFT Method',
    Liturgy, 21(3), 2006, pp. 11-20.
—— and P. Atkins, *Exploring Luke's Gospel: A Guide to the Gospel Readings in
    the Revised Common Lectionary*, London: Mowbray, 2000.
—— and P. Atkins, *Exploring Matthew's Gospel: A Guide to the Gospel Readings
    in the Revised Common Lectionary*, London: Mowbray, 2001.
—— and P. Atkins, *Exploring Mark's Gospel: An Aid for Readers and Preachers
    Using Year B of the Revised Common Lectionary*, London: Continuum,
    2002.
Goldsmith, M. and M. Wharton, *Knowing Me Knowing You*, London: SPCK,
    1993.
Hood, R.W. Jr., P.C. Hill, and W.P. Williams, *The Psychology of Religious
    Fundamentalism*, New York: The Guildford Press, 2005.
Jung, C.G., *Psychological Types: The Collected Works*, vol. VI, London: Rout-
    ledge and Kegan Paul, 1971.
Keirsey, D. and M. Bates, *Please Understand Me*, Del Mar, California: Prome-
    theus Nemesis, 1978.
Myers, I.B. and M.H. McCaulley, *Manual: A Guide to the Development and Use
    of the Myers-Briggs Type Indicator*, Palo Alto, California: Consulting Psy-
    chologists Press, 1985.

Osborn, L. and D. Osborn, *God's Diverse People*. London: Daybreak, 1991.

Vincent, J., ed., *Mark Gospel of Action: Personal and Community Responses*, London: SPCK, 2006.

11

"Be Still" in Barnsley

ALAN SAXBY

In the encroaching darkness of a late autumn afternoon I made my way up a rough farm track to an ancient cottage and barn built into a precipitous South Pennine hillside in "Summer Wine" country, which is the home of the Foster Place Retreat House. Welcomed with a buzz of conversation in its small homely kitchen, I stooped through an appropriately low doorway to progress through a labyrinth of bookshelves exuding a rich seam of spirituality, into the greater space of the old barn and the welcoming warmth of its wood burner. A small group was gathering around a low table on which were a candle, bread and wine.

The occasion was the monthly celebration at the Retreat of what is simply described as an informal Eucharist. True to its origin in a coming together of Christians from the Anglican and Quaker traditions (though not formally sponsored by either), the service begins with a sustained period of silence, which can merge into an experience of stillness before moving to a simple Eucharistic celebration drawing on familiar liturgical patterns. It represents a functional integration of a spirituality that resonates with the emotional and intellectual needs of living in our post-modern 21st century.

A Pilgrimage into Stillness

It was a further step along a personal pilgrimage that had commenced for me about twenty years previously, at a time when the church I attended in Barnsley found itself without a home following the discovery of serious structural weakness in the wall and roof of our magnificent Grade II listed Victorian edifice. This initiated a brief but stimulating period when we were forced to face up to issues of what it meant to be "church" in the late 20th century. The insecurity was too great for some, who withdrew or transferred their membership; for others, it was a straightforward issue of how to rebuild, but for a few of us there was little enthusiasm for exploration of institutional salvation – it seemed more relevant to accept the new situation as a precursor of what was inevitably going to happen in our post-Christian, post-modern society, and to explore experimentally some ways of "being church" in this context. We had no grand master plan, although we did have the sympathetic interest of our then ministers. There was a limited time for innovation before the conventional institutional un-derstandings and procedures regained their self-confidence and moved inexorably towards the re-creation of the widely failing contemporary pattern of "church". Comfortably familiar agendas began to reappear and reassert themselves.

One low profile initiative however did continue with a small group (initially only four people) who agreed to meet together to explore how we might "be" in order that we might "be church" in our every-day lives. With heavy work schedules and family responsibilities, we committed ourselves to meet between 9 and 10 p.m. on a regular Sun-day evening each month. The group, now grown by slow accretion to about a dozen, continues to meet, with a membership that has always been enriched through the presence of those with differing faith com-mitments.

It was on only the second meeting of this group that we began to explore the value of stillness.

This was something I had stumbled across in the preceding years – not in church – initially on a training course related to my work, where we were taken through an extensive process of relaxation to enhance our physical self-awareness, during which I experienced a profound feeling of stillness. Shortly afterward, casually browsing at the bookstall on Sheffield Station, I picked up a paperback book by Her-bert Benson: *The Relaxation Response.*[1] In this, Dr. Benson described how he used relaxation practices in the Harvard Medical School as part of a therapeutic procedure – an approach that also drew on the experi-ence of meditation in the practice of mystics, ancient and modern, in all the world's major religions. It made sense, and I subsequently was able to use this approach alongside complementary techniques on oc-casion in work and church settings, with both groups and individuals, including some outcomes that can only be described in terms of per-sonal healing.

---

[1] Herbert Benson, M.D. with Miriam Z. Klipper, *The Relaxation Response*, rev. ed., New York: Harper Collins, 2000.

Stillness is more than being quiet; it is deeper than silence – although both quiet and silence provide the environment and the way into stillness. Silence is the precondition, and in quietening our physical and mental being (in ways that can be learned), the awareness of stillness begins to infiltrate into consciousness. It is a stillness that wells up from deep within us, and seemingly from beyond, and is a sense that is enhanced when shared with others. Stillness comes as Gift and Grace.

Stillness on a Himalayan Peak

The pre-war Himalayan mountaineer and explorer, Frank Smythe, evocatively describes his experience on achieving the 24,000 ft summit – alone – of the appropriately named Mana Peak:

> That day there was no wind, not the lightest breathing of the atmosphere, and I knew a silence such as I had never known before. I felt that to shout or talk would be profane and terrible, that this silence would shatter in dreadful ruin about me, for it was not the silence of man or earth but the silence of space and eternity. I strained my ears and heard – nothing. Yet, even as I strained, I was conscious of something greater than silence, a Power, the presence of an absolute and immutable Force, so that I seemed on the very boundary of things knowable and unknowable.[2]

As the Psalmist reminded us, albeit in rather negative fashion (Ps 139.7-12), we do not need to ascend Mana Peak to experience that silence which begins to speak of so much more, nor to devote ourselves to the extreme disciplines of many mystical practitioners encountered within a range of world faiths. Many ordinary people have encountered such moments of awareness and realisation, and many ordinary people within different traditions have learned to value the practice of stillness within their faith-pilgrimage.

Stilling the Storm (Mark 4.35–5.1)

In marking GCSE Religious Studies papers on the life and teaching of Jesus, I became familiar with the categorisation of Mark's account of Jesus stilling the storm as a "nature miracle" – yet I suspect that readers over the centuries (certainly if the evidence of our hymnody is any guide) have always sensed more existential meanings, given the power

---

[2] "The Valley of Flowers", in Frank Smythe, *The Six Alpine/Himalayan Climbing Books*, Baton Wicks. Quoted in *The Great Outdoors*, April 2001.

of the storm image to express some of our most disturbing experiences, whether psychological or social, individual or community.

It is a valid instinct for, from its earliest expression, this story has never been a simplistic "wow" story to buttress belief, but has embedded within it mythic elements that connect with its hearers/ readers both then and now.

In the early period of modern biblical criticism, rationalists homed in on the absurdity of a group of fishermen in their home waters being in such a state of panic when having to deal with a familiar problem, and turning to a carpenter for help (though perhaps to help bale out instead of sleeping?). Rationalism suggested that the real miracle was in the calming presence of Jesus, stilling the internal panic of his disciples, enabling them to take control once more of themselves and hence of their situation through using the skills and experience of years to bring the boat safe home to port. It is a reading that has distinct value, but has the deficiency of failing to recognise the profound mythic element within Mark's story-telling.

Jesus commands the storm to "Be still", using (in Greek) the very same word he had uttered to silence the demon in the Capernaum synagogue (Mark 1.25). Jesus confronts the storm as if it were a pack of demons!

For the Jew of the late Second Temple period, the sea was the natural home of demons, the place where the primeval forces of chaos arose from the deep, provoking fear and anxiety. The Psalmist exults:

> You rule the raging of the sea;
> when its waves rise, you still them. (Ps 89.9)

In the very next story Mark relates, when demons were expelled from the Gerasene demoniac they asked for a home in a herd of swine (an appropriate body), who in a consequent fit of madness destroyed themselves in the sea (where the demons were "home") (Mark 5.2–13).

Hence it is no surprise that in the vision of the New Jerusalem (Rev 21.1), it is recorded that "the sea was no more."

That word "Be still" brought calm to the turmoil raging around them, subdued the fears and anxieties that threatened to overwhelm, and replaced the clamour of the storm with "a great calm": restoring the harmony of creation where the forces of primeval chaos were asserting their presence. And so it was with those described in first century terms as possessed of demons: the word "Be still" brought healing and restored harmony to those whose lives were disrupted and disturbed within a society under stress as it was confronted by rapid economic, social and cultural change.[3] An experience not confined to the first century.

I wonder if Jesus had to raise his voice above the noise of the storm, or if he spoke with a tone of quiet, firm authority? A "still, small voice of calm"?

Stillness and Stress

Human life is fragile, although in our modern Western society we are largely protected from the most basic anxieties of sustenance and survival by our control of the world economic system coupled with a complex social organisation.

One of the most fundamental human reactions to experiences of threat is what is known as the "Fight or Flight" response. It is the raising of the fur on the neck of a cat when faced by its canine adversary. It is the tensing of the muscles, the change in breathing patterns and in heart rate as the organism (human or animal) prepares to deal with the threat (real or imagined) it faces. And all that energy is then discharged in either the "fight" or the "flight".

Whilst responding to challenge is an essential element in human growth and development, the difficulty in our modern society is that the challenges and demands that we have to face up and confront in our daily living don't have that clear definition that our prehistoric ancestors presumably faced. Threats today are often more subtle, internal, and psychologically or socially conditioned. Although real physical danger can confront us at any time, for many of us the threats and anxieties that gnaw away at our sense of comfort, well-being, self-worth and happiness on a daily basis arise mainly from issues of relationship, position, status and recognition, from the anxieties of mounting bills and "making ends meet", or from the sheer uncertainty and ambiguity of much that is going on around us (frequently reinforced by our 24/7 news culture).

The anxiety, challenge or threat stimulates our "fight or flight" mechanisms but, unlike our ancestors, we have no clear way of discharging that thrusting energy.

Energetic activity, alcohol and drug abuse, music, sport (spectator or participant) are amongst many common ways of differing value for releasing this energy. Yet, a significant part of that undischarged energy

---

[3] R.A. Horsley, *Jesus and the Spiral of Violence: Popular Jewish Resistance in Roman Palestine*, San Francisco: Harper and Row, 1987, pp. 154-55, 184-90; John Dominic Crossan, *The Historical Jesus: The Life of a Mediterranean Jewish Peasant*, Edinburgh: T. & T. Clark, 1991, pp. 313-18.

can also become either internalised or loosed onto those around us – either way damaging both our inner selves and the fabric of the network of social relationships that surrounds and supports us. Its effect on the health (especially hypertension and all that can flow from that) is well documented. In the sense of an energy within that is unfocussed, unrecognised and uncontrolled, it could almost be described as the "demonic within". But it is a part of that much broader and all-pervasive experience of stress that is a marked feature of our present world, albeit experienced very differently by people in line with their roles and status in society.

Stillness and Healing

In *The Relaxation Response*, Benson sets out the evidence that has underpinned his work at Harvard. He argues that there is a "Relaxation Response" which is the body's natural antidote to "Fight or Flight". It is accompanied by measurable physiological changes and is a response that we can learn how to bring into play. In his medical practice it is combined with other established therapeutic processes.

A significant part of Benson's thesis is concerned with contemporary experience and practice in meditation, as well as drawing on the traditions of mysticism found in the major world religions, identifying commonalities of practice and associated descriptions of inner spiritual experience.

This links closely with the practice and experience of stillness which offers a process of healing, releasing the God-given healing energy deep within us all, facilitating a restoration of balance and harmony for those whose essential being is distorted and stressed by the pressures and demands of our contemporary world (which is pretty well all of us!).

This is not escape from the world – it is renewal for engaging the world.

Stillness in a Post-Modern World

During this period of discovery, our local church was also moving on. It became part of a larger church (on the usual "bigger is beautiful" thesis) through amalgamations. As often happens, however, this did break open some patterns of being that were much too set in stone. One such indicator of openness to change was a policy of structuring in different styles of worship on a Sunday. The suggestion was floated by a colleague that our journeying into stillness might find a wider echo in this new context.

Yet, how do we share something radically new (for many) within a context of traditional familiarity? A lot of thought and mental visualisation with occasional conversation ensued over a two-year period until we tentatively were able to introduce in the 9.15 a.m. "Early Morning Worship" a bi-monthly service based around the experiencing of stillness. There was a good response from the small congregation – "we should do this every month" was a typical comment – and a year later the church's Worship Consultation supported its establishment as the first service in every month, under the titling of *'Be Still'*.

'Be Still' is about 40 minutes in length, is centred around a five-minute period of stillness, excludes a sermon, but otherwise has a structure with which most worshippers would feel familiar and comfortable. It is the style of approach rather than the content that is important. The preparation and layout of the worship space takes thought, including centralising symbols – a lighted candle being particularly useful. The lectionary reading (usually the Gospel) for the day is read, with just a few words of explanation or reflection prefacing or following to aid its understanding. There is no attempt to impose an interpretation. Likewise, there is no attempt made to include all the elements of worship that are normally looked for within a preaching service – the "agenda" of *'Be Still'* is narrower and more focussed. Prayers from our *Methodist Worship Book* frame the intercessions, and we have found its Collects open to more flexible use, often as opening and closing prayers. We use the traditional hymn book, but seek to make creative use of familiar hymns in ways that will encourage us to focus more on their words; for example, we will use a selection of verses rather than the whole hymn, and employ a mix of reading and singing. We try to be guided by what I describe as the internal liturgical structure of the hymn itself – its usage of I/we, its combinations of affirmations and supplications, etc.

Crucially, *'Be Still'* is not a "Preaching Service" with its demand for exposition and proclamation, which is inherently "modern" rather than "post-modern" in its conceptualisation, being framed within the discourse of "Thus saith the Lord". *'Be Still'* is self-consciously post-modern, offering a blend of texts from the rich stream of devotion we have inherited, both ancient and modern – liturgical, hymnic, scripture – for reflection and response. Each is enabled to hear, reflect, understand and respond in their own way. And it is a blending of these devotional streams framing the sharing of that period of silence which, merging into stillness, encourages us to sense, perhaps momentarily, that Presence which undergirds the universe.

Involving a different mind-set from that involved in the preparation and delivery of the Liturgy of the Word, whether in "contemporary" or "traditional" format, this style of approach to worship requires different preparation and training. Fortunately it is simpler, and we are developing and equipping a small team of people to help further pilot this development and embed it in the life of the congregation.

As such, it is an approach that is eminently transferable into many other contexts.

We are experiencing a very slow but steady growth in this congregation, now about thirty in strength, with a good spread of ages, and a typical response on leaving is "Thank you. I needed that!"

Renewed, through stillness, we return to the world to live the gospel.

"Be still" is not the command for awesome obeisance "with reverence and with fear" before an overpowering Deity, as in the very popular modern hymn by David Evans; it is the gently growing awareness that is beyond words of that Presence which draws us together at depth into itself and is better expressed through the words of the Quaker, John Greenleaf Whittier:

> Drop thy still dews of quietness,
> Till all our strivings cease;
> Take from our souls the strain and stress,
> And let our ordered lives confess
> The beauty of thy peace.
>
> Breathe through the heats of our desire
> Thy coolness and thy balm;
> Let sense be dumb, let flesh retire;
> Speak through the earthquake, wind, and fire,
> O still small voice of calm!

12

Time for Jesus to Wake Up

GERALD WEST AND BONGI ZENGELE

A foundational commitment of liberation theology has been to grant the poor and marginalised an epistemological privilege.[1] What this means is that the particular understandings, experiences, and concerns of the poor and marginalised communities are the starting point and the immersion place for the reading of the Bible and the doing of theology. Liberation theologies have been attentive to class, race, gender, ethnicity, sexual orientation, and other features of marginalisation over the past forty years. And while HIV and AIDS have yet to become a distinct feature of a theology of liberation, being HIV-positive and living with AIDS in many contexts is to be stigmatised and discriminated against, whether by ones family, ones church, ones government, or society more generally.

In this essay we will reflect on some of the incipient and embryonic theology that is beginning to emerge among support groups of South Africans who are living positively with HIV and AIDS. The reflections we will share all come from the network of Siyaphila ("We are alive!") support groups that have emerged in KwaZulu-Natal, the epicentre of the HIV epidemic in South Africa, in the wake of the HIV epidemic, as they have worked together with the Ujamaa Centre.[2] The Ujamaa Centre, a community development and research centre located in the School of Religion and Theology in the University of KwaZulu-Natal in South Africa, works with the Bible among communities of the poor,

---

[1] Per Frostin, *Liberation Theology in Tanzania and South Africa: A First World Interpretation*, Lund: Lund University Press, 1988, p. 10.

[2] Gerald O. West, "Reading the Bible in the Light of HIV/Aids in South Africa," *The Ecumenical Review* 55.4, 2003.

marginalised, and working-class, collaborating with them to use the Bible as a resource for God's project of survival, liberation, and life.[3]

The two most prominent forms of theology which have emerged from Siyaphila groups have been, first, a theology of resilience and hope in the face of relentless stigma and discrimination. Here the gospel texts in which Jesus takes a stand on the side of the poor and marginalised over against the religious, political, and economic leadership have been their primary sources for doing theology.[4] The second prominent form of theology has been a theology of lament, and here the Psalms and the book of Job have been substantial resources.[5]

Another less explicit form of theology can also be discerned. We are not sure what to call this incipient theology, but in the remainder of this essay we will try to capture some of its contours.

A Contextual Bible Study

What has come to be called "Contextual Bible Study" is the product of nearly twenty years of praxis, primarily the praxis of the South African context, but shaped too by the praxis of the Brasilian Centro de Estudos Bíblicos (CEBI).[6] Briefly, Contextual Bible Study accepts and affirms that the Bible is a significant and sacred resource in the South African context, particularly among poor, working-class, and marginalised sectors. Occupying the interface between the multifarious resources such sectors already have for interpreting the Bible and the structured and systematic "critical" resources of biblical scholarship, Contextual Bible Study facilitates an engagement and exchange between these related but different sets of resources, with the explicit purpose of participating in God's emancipatory project by working towards social and personal transformation. Within the epistemological framework described above, the typical structure of a Contextual Bible Study begins with an open-ended engagement with the biblical text, encouraging participants to bring their reception history to the interpretation of a particular text. This is followed by a series of initially literary and then socio-historical questions, which are designed to

[3] West, "Contextual Bible Reading: A South African Case Study", *Analecta Bruxellensia* 11, 2006; West, *The Academy of the Poor: Towards a Dialogical Reading of the Bible*. Pietermaritzburg: Cluster Publications, 2003.

[4] West, "Reading the Bible in the Light of HIV/Aids in South Africa".

[5] Gerald O. West and Bongi Zengele, "Reading Job 'Positively' in the Context of HIV/Aids in South Africa," *Concilium* 4, 2004; Gerald O. West, "The Poetry of Job as a Resource for the Articulation of Embodied Lament in the Context of HIV and Aids in South Africa," in *Lamentations in Ancient and Contemporary Cultural Contexts*, Nancy C. Lee and Carleen Mandolfo, eds., Atlanta: Society of Biblical Literature, 2008.

[6] Carlos A. Dreher, *The Walk to Emmaus*. Sao Leopoldo: Centro de Estudios Bíblicos, 2004.

probe the biblical text in a structured and systematic manner but which are phrased in an accessible and simple way. The Contextual Bible Study then comes to its conclusion through a final series of questions which relate the structured and systematic reading of scripture to the particular concerns of the community, as already determined by their own analysis of their reality.

This format of biblical interpretation has been embraced and adopted by the Siyaphila support groups.[7] Among the many Bible studies they have done in their rhythm of fortnightly Contextual Bible Study is a Bible study on Mark 4.35–5.1. The Bible study took the following shape:

Question 1:	Retell the story in your own words in "buzz groups" of two. What is the text about?
Question 2:	Who is sailing the boat, and what is Jesus doing in the boat?
Question 3:	When and why do the disciples wake Jesus?
Question 4:	What are they afraid of?
Question 5:	What are we who are living with HIV and AIDS afraid of?
Question 6:	Is Jesus in "the boat" with those living with HIV and AIDS? If he is, is he asleep or awake?
Question 7:	If Jesus is still asleep, how do we wake him up?
Question 8:	If he is awake or if he were to waken, what would we want him to do?
Question 9:	What does this story challenge us to do?

Question 1 opens up space for the group members to share whatever their impressions of this text might be. It is an important question because it establishes that anyone in the group may participate and that any response is acceptable. This question makes it evident, even to new members, that the facilitator is just that, a facilitator and not the "expert" voice. Once participants realise that they really can make a contribution, with every response being recognised (and often recorded publicly on newsprint by the group "scribe"), there is a flurry of responses, with most of the members saying something.

Questions 2, 3, and 4 return the participants to the biblical text. In this case there is no in-depth probing of the literary features of the text or of the world behind the text, as there is in many other Contextual Bible Studies.[8] Here the readers simply return to read the text again, giving the text its own voice, and affirming that the text does indeed have a voice.

---

[7] West, "Reading the Bible in the Light of HIV/Aids in South Africa."
[8] West, "Contextual Bible Reading: A South African Case Study."

Questions 5, 6, 7, and 8 then shift back again to the readers' reality, in an overtly contextual reading, ending the process with an action plan.

This is a Contextual Bible Study which has been forged by ordinary readers of the Bible, with the support of an organic intellectual, Bongi Zengele, and a socially engaged biblical scholar, Gerald West, both from the Ujamaa Centre. While it follows the contours of the Contextual Bible Study methodology, it does not draw heavily on the resources of critical biblical scholarship. But it does respect the text, providing an opportunity between the two moments of engagement (between Question 1 and Questions 5–8) to re-read the text.

Question 1 generates a host of responses, ranging from answers like: faith, fear, anxiety, the power of God, a miracle, Jesus teaching his disciples, etc. Question 2 often elicits some surprise, as participants notice that it is the disciples who are in control of the boat, not Jesus. They are the ones with expertise in sailing, not Jesus. This detail becomes significant later, when they respond to Question 6, 7, and 8, all of which emphasise the agency of the participants (all of whom are HIV-positive). Some participants notice that Jesus is asleep "on the cushion", and wonder why Mark has given us this particular detail. Perhaps, some suggest, this is to reassure us that Jesus is only unaware of the danger facing the disciples because he is so comfortable. Jesus is not uncaring. He is exhausted by his teaching and so has fallen asleep, but without the pillow he would probably have woken by himself as the boat became more and more violently shaken by the wind and the waves. Others venture that Jesus is being uncaring, making himself comfortable while the disciples struggle with the task of sailing the boat in increasingly difficult conditions.

Question 3, with its dual focus, reflects on how the disciples only wake Jesus when the situation is no longer in their control, when "the boat was already being swamped" (v. 37), in the expectation that he might or will be able to help them. Jesus is significant, and at times just his presence is enough, without his active involvement; but at other times he is expected or required to act in a form of participation that exceeds presence.

Question 4 already begins to shift the readers, in most cases, to their own realities, for there is not much in the text to interrogate with regard to this question. Obviously they were afraid of dying (v. 38), but perhaps their fear was heightened by the very presence of Jesus with them. Perhaps they felt some responsibility for him, for he was not, after all, a fisherman, and so would not be familiar with this kind of situation. But more importantly he was their leader, and so there was the weight of responsibility to protect him. Furthermore, Jesus had given their lives new meaning and so to die now, with him, was a situation worthy of dread. These reflections, however, are intimately linked to the fears of Siyaphila members, who fear not only for their own lives but also for the lives of those for whom they are responsible, particularly their children. They too have discovered a new sense of "life" (*ukuphila*) since their diagnosis as HIV-positive, especially since they joined the Siyaphila support group.

The shift to the readers' realities is decisive in Question 5, moving directly from text to participants' contexts. Those living with HIV and AIDS have much to fear. Our government is only gradually rolling out antiretroviral (ARV) treatment, so not everyone who needs ARVs is able to obtain them at the appropriate time. Even when we are able to access ARVs, the stigma associated with taking the medication is as severe as the stigma associated with being HIV-positive. Added to this is the fear of not having sufficient nutritious food to allow the body to cope with the toxic ARV drugs. Then there is the fear that one's body will develop resistance to the particular cocktails available in our country, where we do not yet have second or third generation drugs (as western countries do). But the deepest fear is not living long enough to see one's children go to school or to be reconciled and accepted by one's family. As one Siyaphila member wrote after our Contextual Bible Study on Job 3:

> God you have allowed me to feel this painful experience. I don't know whether this is because I am a bad person in your eyes, or because of my sinfulness. You have taken away my husband, I am left alone with four young children to look after and I am unemployed. My prayer is: please help me to raise these children under your guidance, let them do good in your eyes like Job. I am begging you to keep me alive for a longer time so that I can be there for my children. Give me strength to come closer to you, more than before God. I curse the family (my in-laws) I stay with, they are horrible to me![9]

Question 6 is perhaps the pivotal question. This question is, indeed, the question around which the whole Bible study is based, derived as it is from the discussions among Siyaphila members of this text before the Contextual Bible Study itself was developed. In informal reflections around this text, Bongi Zengele heard one of the discussants declare that "It is time for Jesus to wake up!" Probing, she discovered that this is what some of them felt when they read this text, though they were not sure they should feel or say such things about Jesus. And so the seed of a Contextual Bible Study was sown. Question 6 opens up for-

---

[9] West, "The Poetry of Job as a Resource for the Articulation of Embodied Lament in the Context of HIV and Aids in South Africa."

mal space, within the safe, sacred site of a Siyaphila Bible study, to delve more deeply into this embodied cry: "It is time for Jesus to wake up!"

Question 7 continues to encourage the participants to do theology, invoking our own participation in God's work. In earlier Bible studies on the book of Job,[10] some of the Siyaphila groups had explored aspects of the book of Job in which God might be considered to argue that God's work is not yet complete, that there are dimensions to creation that remain unresolved, as is evident when we "Look at Behemoth" (40.15) or when we consider Leviathan (41.1).[11]

Questions 8 and 9 move the Contextual Bible Study to its conclusion, inviting participants to envisage and plan for transformation. We usually ask participants to work towards concrete "action plans", beginning with an immediate action that can be taken, then planning an action that requires some additional time and resources but which is nevertheless feasible within their context, and finally to imagine a plan of action that might be possible if there were appropriate resources.

From Embodied Theology to Public Theology

What emerges in Contextual Bible Studies such as this, if the group is a sacred and safe space,[12] is that the embodied theologies of the participants find forms of articulation.[13] Such emergent articulations are what South African theologian James Cochrane calls "incipient theology".[14] Incipient theology is a product of the corporate/embodied experience of the group, who draw both on the resources of their own bodies and the biblical text to bring to articulation what is inchoate. So in this case, though this same group of people have affirmed in other Contextual Bible Studies that Jesus stands with them over against stigmatising society, they are also able to bring to words another part of their lived reality, namely a Jesus who is in some senses asleep. And, as they said, "It is time for Jesus to wake up"! Here are the beginnings of a profound theology of both God's presence and absence in the context of HIV and AIDS!

---

[10] Ibid.

[11] Cf. L.G. Perdue, *Wisdom in Revolt: Metaphorical Theology in the Book of Job*, Sheffield: Almond Press, 1991.

[12] Cf. James C. Scott, *Domination and the Arts of Resistance: Hidden Transcripts*, New Haven and London: Yale University Press, 1990.

[13] While sharing some of these ideas with theological students in Chennai, India, they preferred the phrase "embodied theology" for what we had up to that point called "lived" or "working theology". We have taken up their term.

[14] James R. Cochrane, *Circles of Diginity: Community Wisdom and Theological Reflection*, Minneapolis: Fortress, 1999.

As South African theologian Albert Nolan has argued, the socially engaged biblical scholar and theologian are called to serve such communities and their incipient theologies.[15] We are called to collaborate with groups like the Siyaphila network, placing ourselves and our resources alongside them and their resources, working together to give theological form to what is already a lived reality. Such collaboration produces forms of local theology which can be articulated and owned by those to whom it is organic.

But the socially engaged theologians' task is not yet done. For a final challenge remains, that of in/corporating local theologies such as this into the public theologies of the institutional church.[16] In/corporation is not uncritical, for implicit in the process of articulation, owning and in/corporation is, as Cochrane has argued, a communitarian and critical component.

First, embodied theologies, as "symbolic structures", arise out of, and are situated in, the strongly communitarian life world of the community, including both the living and the living dead. Second, the discourses of the Bible study, particularly the constructive engagement between local and scholarly reading resources, "bring to the group's attention selected aspects of the taken-for-granted, shared background knowledge of its life world. These aspects move to the foreground, becoming conscious". Third, "this move to the foreground of previously unreflected elements of the life world introduces the possibility of questioning and probing", that is, a critical component. Fourth, the mode of discourse in the Bible studies, including both the facilitation and the interaction between contextual and textual questions, promotes and establishes "a process of communication that allows for open argument and counterargument as the basis for testing claims made". Fifth, this process makes possible "an encounter between traditions (biblically transmitted tradition, local group tradition, and more generally, aspects of African tradition) in the context of a social environment shaped by severe negative imbalances in material resources and access to power". Though the emphasis in the articulation and owning of embodied theologies is corporate, included in this encounter between traditions are also the "personal dimensions in both tradition and everyday life". Sixth, it is this encounter between the personal and the corporate, Cochrane argues, that establishes potential links "between

---

[15] Albert Nolan, "Work, the Bible, Workers, and Theologians: Elements of a Workers' Theology", *Semeia* 73, 1996.

[16] We are grateful to two colleagues, Pat Bruce and Steve de Gruchy, for suggesting this use of "in/corporate", which draws on the root "corpus", meaning body, and which therefore makes a nice connection between embodied theologies and the need to have them in/corporated, that is, brought into the body of the church.

the cultural, social, and personal elements of the life world" as participants in the Bible study endeavour "to understand what a claim made
in one sphere, for example, concerning personal responsibility for theft,
might imply for another sphere, for example, the struggle against poverty".[17]

Underlying this entire process, then, is what Cochrane refers to as
the "communicative rationality" of local knowledge and theologies.[18]
Embodied theologies that have been articulated and owned are a form
of corporate communicative rationality, and as such can be and, I am
arguing here, must be communicatively shared. "A public theology
that does not take the perspective of local communities of the poor,
the oppressed, and the marginalized seriously loses its seminal sources
of insight and correction".[19]

We have leaned heavily on Cochrane's work because it is the most
pragmatically suggestive and theoretically coherent account we know
of; that it emerges from the South African context increases its potential usefulness for the realities we have identified. The Ujamaa Centre
will continue to use the Bible – and to train others to use the Bible –
as a resource for the articulation and owning of embodied theologies.
We will also continue to urge Siyaphila members to remain cognisant
of and connected to their embodied theologies, even though they may
yet lack the resources for giving coherent articulation to them. We will
do this while we wait for those theologically better equipped than we
are to come alongside us "to do theology", both at the local and at the
public level.

In advocating for embodied theologies, we are not denigrating all
that we find in the public realm of theology. There is much there of
value, fashioned and forged as it has been by centuries of action and
reflection. But we want us to recognise the desperateness of our current South African context, in which many Christians find little to
guide or nourish them. We are concerned by the migratory behaviour
of so many Christians who set out by day (to one church) and by night
(to another church) to seek out pastures new, yearning for good news.
Unless we find some way of connecting their embodied theologies and
the public theologies of their churches, they will continue to wander
in a wilderness of public theologies that do not resonate with their
lived experience.

---

[17] Cochrane, *Circles of Diginity: Community Wisdom and Theological Reflection*, p. 128.

[18] Ibid., pp. 28, 132.

[19] Ibid., p. 124. Cochrane goes on to consider an ecclesiology appropriate to this
analysis; cf. *Circles of Diginity: Community Wisdom and Theological Reflection*, pp. 132-49.

Conclusion

Under the dried crust of our often bereft public theology resides a deeper, usually unarticulated and incipient, theology. This embodied theology has been generated by our lived faith and experiences, but it is inchoate and unformed. A challenge that awaits the church is to draw deeply from this rich residual substratum of theology and to bring it into the public realm. Only then will the church be the kind of safe and sacred space where women, people living with HIV and AIDS, those marginalised and abused by society, and the poor, are fully at home.

What is more, only then will the church be the body of Christ. Only then will Jesus be awake.

13

Waking the Lively Dead Man

IAN WALLIS

Every church community inherits Jesus sleeping in the stern. How he got there no-one quite remembers. In fact, the existence of the boat is equally inexplicable. As is the crew among whom we find ourselves numbered and the voyage on which we're set. We trust all this once made sense and was persuasive. That, awake, Jesus demanded attention and attracted supporters willing to venture beyond familiar waters in pursuit of God's kingdom causes. But none of the original recruits survives, not even their successors. And the vessel has been en route for so many generations that the Galilean shoreline from which it embarked is barely visible, a distant speck on history's horizon. Speculation over where the boat is heading and the purpose of the journey fills the airwaves. And the only person able to supply an answer remains dead to the world.

Apart from a few self-styled passengers, most of us were recruited long before we could remember or were in a position to decide. Yet, for all our remonstrations, we have grown to acknowledge the authority of the one ultimately responsible for our being on board. Perhaps, that's the way it has to be for, from the moment maternal instincts launch us into life, we struggle to inhabit the personae in which epic stories cast us. Mothers are not chosen (nor are families for that matter), yet they define us beyond measure and relate to us beyond sentiment or reason. Baptism is little different – another rite of passage through which we inherit an identity and vocation, this time within the crew of the captain of salvation (Heb 2.10) who bids us sail with him.

"Let us go across to the other side."

Many commentators recognise in Mark's relating of the stilling of the storm (Mark 4.35–41) a veiled reference to mission as the message of Jesus reaches out to the Gentile world. And this centrifugal impetus to share Jesus with others remains the vocation and constant challenge of Christian communities in every generation. For one such gathering, this led them back to the font where they rediscovered something of the missionary potential of baptism.

St Michael and All Angels is the Anglican parish church in the centre of an ex-mining township called Houghton-le-Spring, on the outskirts of Sunderland in the North-East of England. For all the changes (not least in demography) that have taken place since the closure of the colliery back in 1982, many of its residents still look to the church when key life events expand their humanity beyond the ordinary and, for that reason, need navigating and marking in appropriate ways.

The birth of a child is one such occasion. Most Monday evenings, the vestry would be visited by mums (sometimes accompanied by dads) bearing their babies. They'd come to have them "done". It's a journey repeated in parishes throughout the Christian world and yet how readily we overlook its enormity. People unfamiliar with the practices and beliefs of organised religion who may never have attended a service of worship, unsure of how they will be received, make their way "to the other side". What a remarkable expression of nascent faith every bit as significant as, for instance, that of the woman whose chronic haemorrhaging caused her to burrow through the crowds in search of wholeness (Mark 5.25–34).

Unsurprisingly, few are able to give account of their faith, to articulate it in religious techno-speak, for it is what they lack or long for that has drawn them. And how often do they encounter a dormant Jesus, asleep in the stern, in the form of suspicious looks, awkward questions and a string of demands. But what else do they expect, we protest? After all, baptism is the rite of Christian initiation. How can you seek baptism for your child if you know next to nothing about Jesus and have little desire to belong to a church community? Surely, it is for their own good that we put them through courses of preparation and mandatory church attendance before granting their request.

It all sounds so reasonable, so responsible and, according to the new initiation liturgies of the Church of England and many other denominations, so necessary. But is it gospel? Are we not in danger of stemming the radical gratuitousness of Jesus who, when approached by those who knew little about him and demonstrated even less of a desire to follow him, proffered a healing touch, a forgiving word or a generous welcome? And is not such radical gratuitousness the means by which we come to see ourselves in a different light? These are some of the questions the staff and congregation of St Michael's began to ask.

And leaving the crowd behind, they took him with them in the boat, just as he was. Other boats were with him. A great windstorm arose, and the waves beat into the boat, so that the boat was already being swamped.

Although precipitated by the approaches of those from "the other side", we at St Michael's soon found ourselves plunged once more into the waters of our own baptism as we grappled with its meaning. These proved to be turbulent times when we struggled to listen to one another and embrace the diversity of experience and understanding which surfaced. We studied the baptismal practices of the early Christians and explored the complex relationships between divine initiative and human response, as well as between ritual and reality. We retraced our own journeys of faith back to the font, revisiting significant cairns along the way and giving thanks for those who embodied Christ's life for us and nurtured us in the same.

And through all our reflecting, remembering and soul-searching, one biblical image emerged as the vessel capable of carrying our aspirations, experiences and beliefs:

> Jesus said to Nicodemus, "Very truly, I tell you, no-one can see the kingdom of God without being born again." Nicodemus said to him, "How can anyone be born after having grown old? Can one enter a second time into the mother's womb and be born?" Jesus answered, "Very truly, I tell you, no-one can enter the kingdom of God without being born of water and Spirit. What is born of the flesh is flesh, and what is born of the Spirit is spirit." (John 3.3–5; cf. Titus 3.4–5)

Baptism as new birth. Here was an insight we could all relate to and one which we found to be overflowing with surpluses of meaning. It spoke to us of baptism as a precious gift and one which, like life itself, has nothing to do with us (we do not create life) and yet has everything to do with us (we are the life created). A gift that can be seen as an initial investment, full of potential, which, given conducive conditions, will yield growth, maturity and fulfilment. One that is offered graciously, but which only truly becomes a gift when recognised and lived out as such.

Here was an image of baptism that celebrated the God of Life, whose fathomless resourcefulness is the ground of our being both human and Christian, whilst inviting us to inhabit the freedoms and responsibilities, the identity and the vocation, intrinsic to being a new creation, a child of God and disciple of Christ. That Easter, we returned to the font to reaffirm our faith with a fresh appreciation of baptism as the beginning of a life-long journey on which we become whom we already are as we grow into the fullness of our God-given humanity in the company of Jesus and the community gathering in his name.

But he was in the stern, asleep on the cushion; and they woke him up and said to him, "Teacher, do you not care that we are perishing?" He woke up and rebuked the wind, and said to the sea, "Peace! Be still!" Then the wind ceased, and there was a dead calm. He said to them, "Why are you afraid? Have you still no faith?"

Revitalised by a fresh overwhelming of God's graciousness, we gained an appetite for sharing something of that generosity with those seeking baptism for their children. Vestry hour was revamped. The waiting area, which used to resemble a cross between an old-style doctor's reception and the space outside a head-teacher's study, became a place of welcome and hospitality. Church regulars volunteered to greet inquirers and help them feel at home. There were tea and cakes, toys and noise, and lots of fuss over the little ones and support for their parents.

During the meeting with the minister, parents were encouraged to share a little of their stories as well as what brought them to church on this occasion. We introduced the service of thanksgiving for the gift of a child as well as the service of baptism. We explained how both usually took place on a Sunday afternoon and lasted approximately 30 minutes, one family per service, with members of the family of faith also taking part. A simple explanatory leaflet was provided and parents were encouraged to spend a few days thinking about which service reflected where they were and what they were looking for. Although some families were initially phased by this approach, most came to recognise that the church was taking them seriously and seeking to minister appropriately.

Those opting for thanksgiving were relieved that they didn't have to say things they didn't believe, whilst those opting for baptism appreciated the opportunity of having to think through what they were looking for before making a positive choice. Baptism families were also invited to a main Sunday service when they would be welcomed into the community of faith. Invitations to the monthly pram service were extended to all, as were invites to the Christingle and Crib services. Photos of all the little ones were included in the parish magazine as well as displayed at the back of church. Anniversary of baptism cards were sent out to the 70 plus "new recruits" who passed through the waters each year until they were old enough to attend young church when a personalised invitation would be delivered in its place.

He woke up and rebuked the wind, and said to the sea, "Peace! Be still!" Then the wind ceased, and there was a dead calm.

Throughout this stormy and faith-stretching transition, something of the graciousness of God's life incarnated in Jesus, embodied among his followers and celebrated in baptism came to the fore. Those involved in this ministry found themselves caught up in a wave of gratuitousness whilst those on the other side discovered the space to gain a fuller sense of what was being offered. As the months passed, a greater appreciation of the *dynamics of gift* impressed themselves upon us. One question came to the fore, "Can a gift be given?" Experience guided us towards a qualified, "No". For gifts only become gifts when they are received with some recognition of what is being offered and by whom. Otherwise, they remain rights, rewards or plunder. This brought into focus what we came to acknowledge as one of the foremost challenges of mission in the current climate, namely how can we help one another, and especially those whose faith remains dormant, perceive the good things that God offers us in Jesus and receive them as gifts?

Baptism came to life at St Michael's. Not primarily because of needing to formulate a strategy for those seeking a rite of passage for their new arrivals (although this was the initial motivation), but through renewal among the community of the baptised, the congregation, as they began to inhabit the realisation that baptism wasn't something belonging to the past, but something that characterised their present and informed their future. "We are never more than is celebrated at the font" became our watchword, for it is from there that our Christian identity and vocation flows. This, in turn, enthused many of the regulars as they came to see themselves as life-long apprentices of the lively dead man, acquiring the artistry of faith en route – those wholesome habits of practical discipleship (e.g. forgiveness, hospitality, loving, prayer and wisdom).

St Michael's became a more verdant and wholesome community where people discovered something of genuine worth that made a tangible difference to their experience of living, which in turn overflowed into their decisions, employment, relationships, values and aspirations. In truth, into pretty much everything. Not surprisingly, it became more inviting and vital as a result, drawing in people on the shores as well as attracting those inlanders who never thought of themselves as St Michael's angels or anybody else's for that matter. Including, some of the baptism families who came to the realisation that "getting the bairn done" need not simply be an occasion for a family party or an inoculation against bad things happening to their babies, but an invitation to a fuller life.

And they were filled with great awe and said to one another, "Who then is this, that even the wind and the sea obey him?"

One of the consequences of all this was a renewed interest, even passion, for Jesus and his way. Who was this son of man and son of God and what was he up to? And what has he got to do with us today? *Lively Faith* courses were designed on which we donned the sandals of the first disciples as we heeded Jesus' call, witnessed his healings, experienced his forgiveness, delighted in his stories, ate at his table, pondered his teachings, felt his challenges, plotted his betrayal, received his legacy, suffered his passion, mourned his death. And, through doing so, Jesus emerged from the mists of history and became a living presence once more. No longer asleep in the stern, Jesus demanded attention and engendered allegiance.

Index of Modern Authors

Index of Biblical References